SCIENCE IN SECONDS FOR KIDS

Over 100 Experiments You Can Do in Ten Minutes or Less

Jean Potter

JOHN WILEY & SONS, INC.

York • Chichester • Brisbane • Toronto • Singapore

Copyright © 1995 by Jean Potter
Published by John Wiley & Sons, Inc.

Library of Congress Cataloging-in-Publication Data

Potter, Jean.
    Science in seconds for kids : over 100 experiments you can do in
ten minutes or less / Jean Potter.
        p.   cm.
    Includes bibliographical references and index.
    ISBN 0-471-04456-3 (pbk.: alk. paper)
    1. Science—Experiments—Juvenile literature.
[1. Science—Experiments.   2. Experiments.]   I. Title.
Q164..P78   1995
507.8—dc20   94-31443
                                                           AC

Printed in the United States of America

10   9   8   7   6   5   4   3   2   1

This book is dedicated to my dear friend
James H. Harless
in appreciation for his friendship and love for fellow man
and for his significant contributions to the field of education.

Special thanks to:

Robert M. Frostig, science teacher, Horace Mann Junior High School, Charleston, West Virginia.
Michael J. Chovanec, physics teacher; Tobin George, biology teacher; William Fry, science teacher; Hempfield Area High School, Greensburg, Pennsylvania.

Additional thanks to:

Thomas, my husband, for his incredible love and support.
Archie, our Welsh Corgi, for his companionship and friendship.
Shadow, our Russian Blue, for his constant vigil.
Mary, my friend, for love, understanding, and support.
Mom, Dad, Kathy, and Emmett, my family, for so many reasons.
Kate Bradford, my editor, for her expert opinion and advice.

Contents

Colors

Energy

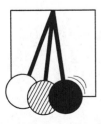

Gravity

The Human Body

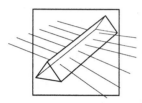

Light

Machines

Magnetism

Magnification

Water

Weather

Introduction

Science in Seconds for Kids contains 108 quick and easy experiments that will help you discover the wonders of science, from how rockets work to what causes lightning. Each activity takes only ten minutes or less to complete. Soon you will be able to look quickly into many exciting topics.

HOW THIS BOOK IS ORGANIZED

Science in Seconds for Kids is divided into sections by topic. If you are looking for a particular activity, you can find it in the Experiment Index at the back of the book.

Each experiment answers a particular question about science and includes a list of the materials you need, easy-to-follow steps, and an explanation of what the experiment demonstrates. There is no need to buy special materials, but you may want to visit the library for additional information on the topic.

TIPS FOR COMPLETING THE EXPERIMENTS

Try to be very careful as you perform your experiments. These tips will help:

Be prepared. Read through any experiment before you begin to do it. Collect all the materials required before you start, and place them in the order in which you will use them. Science can be messy, so wear old clothes while doing experiments. Give yourself enough space to work and enough ventilation. Cover surfaces with newspaper in case of spills.

Be accurate. When conducting your experiments, follow the directions closely, and write down all results. Try repeating the experiment.

Doing the experiment more than once will ensure the accuracy of your results.

Be creative. After completing an experiment according to the directions, try to think of ways that you can change the experiment. Look for the results from your change to the experiment. Before you make the change, ask an adult if your substitution is all right.

Be careful. Ask for adult assistance and supervision when using sharp instruments. Materials should be used for the purpose for which they were intended. Work cautiously.

Be neat. Keep your work and your work area as neat as you can. Use clean instruments, and wash them after every use. Put your materials away after they have been washed.

AIR

Air is a special mixture of gases that surrounds the earth and reaches well into the atmosphere. Since it is colorless, odorless, and tasteless, we sometimes do not remember it is there. But it is, and it is very important.

Air has many uses, from keeping living things alive to making it possible for you to play basketball. In this section, you will do some experiments to learn how air can push objects, lift things, and make balls bounce.

DRY PAPER

Can Paper Stay Dry in Water?

MATERIALS

tap water
plastic tub
sheet of paper
plastic cup

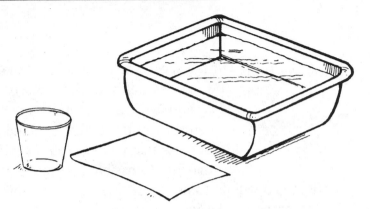

PROCEDURE

1. Run tap water into the plastic tub until the tub is about three-quarters full.

2. Crumple the sheet of paper and push it to the bottom of the plastic cup. Use enough paper so it will stay at the bottom when the cup is upside down.

3. Hold the cup upside down and push it into the water. Be sure to hold the cup straight up and down, not tilted.

4. Pull the cup straight up out of the water and remove the paper. What happens to the paper?

EXPLANATION

The paper did not get wet. Air surrounded the paper in the cup. When you pushed the cup into the water, the air was trapped in the cup. The trapped air pushed back on the water, keeping it from reaching the paper. If you had tilted the cup, the air would have escaped and the water would have taken its place. In that case, the paper would have become wet.

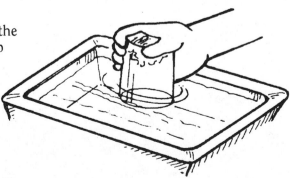

ELASTIC AIR

Why Does a Balloon Filled with Air Bounce?

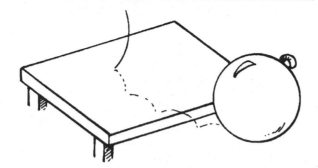

MATERIALS

balloon

PROCEDURE

1. Inflate the balloon.
2. Tie the neck of the balloon closed.
3. With your hand, push in the balloon at different places.
4. Bounce the balloon against a table or the floor. What happens to the balloon when you press or bounce it against something?

EXPLANATION

Balloons are made of an **elastic** (stretchy) material called **latex**. When you blew air into the balloon, the air **molecules** (the smallest particles of a substance that can exist on their own) were packed closer and closer together. When you pushed in on the balloon, you felt the air molecules resisting. The balloon is elastic, and so is the air inside. Because air is elastic, the balloon bounced back when you pushed it against a table or the floor. If the balloon were filled with sand, it would not bounce. This is why basketballs, soccer balls, and other balls are filled with air.

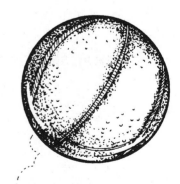

AIR ROCKET
What Happens to Air Under Pressure?

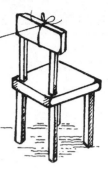

MATERIALS

piece of string about 6 feet (2 m) long
2 chairs
drinking straw
long balloon
masking tape

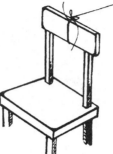

PROCEDURE

1. Tie one end of the piece of string to the first chair.
2. Lace the string through the drinking straw.
3. Tie the other end of the string to the second chair.
4. Move the chairs apart so the string is stretched tight.
5. Inflate the balloon and hold the neck so that no air escapes.
6. Keep the neck of the balloon closed as you tape the balloon to the straw.
7. When the balloon is taped, release the neck. What happens?

EXPLANATION

The balloon was forced along the string. When you inflated the balloon, you pushed air into it. The elastic skin of the balloon put **pressure,** or **force,** on the air inside the balloon. When you released the balloon, the air rushed out with a force that pushed the balloon in the opposite direction. When a rocket is launched, tremendous force is required to lift it off the ground. The rocket gets this force from fuel, which is **ignited** (set on fire) and explodes out the end of the rocket, pushing the rocket up.

AIR PUSH

How Strong Is Air Pressure?

MATERIALS

5-by-8-inch index card
plastic cup
tap water
bowl

PROCEDURE

1. Make sure the index card is large enough to completely cover the top of the plastic cup.
2. Fill the cup with tap water to the brim so that no air space remains.
3. Place the index card on top of the cup. Make sure there is no air between the card and the water. If there is air space, remove the card, add more water, and replace the card.
4. Hold the card in place by putting one hand on it.
5. Turn the cup upside down over the bowl and slowly remove your hand from under the card.
6. Turn the cup slowly in a variety of ways. Can you make the card stay on the glass when you move it in different directions?

EXPLANATION

The air that surrounds us pushes in all directions. Air was pushing against the cup when the cup was right-side up. When you turned the cup upside down, the air maintained its pressure on the index card and held it in place. The card will stay pressed against the cup until a force stronger than air moves it.

AIR SUPPORT

How Does the Shape of an Object Affect How the Object Falls Through the Air?

MATERIALS

scissors
ruler
8-foot (2.4-m) piece of string
2 square handkerchiefs
2 clothespins

PROCEDURE

1. Cut the piece of string into eight 1-foot (30-cm) lengths.
2. Tie a big knot in the middle of one handkerchief.
3. Tie one length of string to each corner of each handkerchief.
4. Gather the ends of the loose strings leading from each handkerchief and tie them in a knot around the head of each clothespin.
5. Grip the center of each handkerchief and toss both handkerchiefs into the air. What happens?

EXPLANATION

The handkerchief knotted in the middle fell to earth faster than the unknotted handkerchief. When an object falls through the air, it hits air molecules. Each molecule pushes up slightly on the falling object. Because the unknotted handkerchief was able to spread out, it caught more air molecules, which slowed its fall.

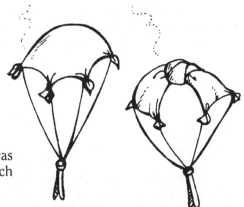

BOTTLE BALLOON

What Happens to Air As It Is Heated and Cooled?

MATERIALS

balloon
2-liter soda bottle
hot tap water
2 cake pans
ice tap water
adult helper

PROCEDURE

1. Fit the balloon over the mouth of the soda bottle.
2. Ask your adult helper to pour the hot water into the first cake pan.
3. Pour the ice water into the second pan.
4. Place the bottle with the balloon in the pan of hot water for a few seconds and observe what happens.
5. Remove the bottle from the hot water and place it in the ice water. What happens to the balloon this time?

EXPLANATION

The bottle looked empty, but was filled with air molecules. These molecules constantly moved around inside the bottle. The hotter the molecules, the more they move and the more room they occupy. When you put the bottle with the balloon over the hot water, the balloon **inflated,** or expanded with air, because the air molecules occupied more space. When you put the bottle with the balloon over the ice water, the balloon **deflated,** or collapsed, because the molecules moved closer together and occupied less space.

BOOK LIFT

Can Air Lift Heavy Objects?

MATERIALS

plastic shopping bag
book

PROCEDURE

1. Place the shopping bag on a table.
2. Place the book on the bag.
3. Arrange the bag so the open end extends off the table. The book should not extend off the table.
4. Lifting the bag a little, blow very hard into the open end. What happens to the book?

EXPLANATION

When you blew into the bag, the book rose off the table. The extra air molecules you added to the bag pushed against each other, causing the bag to expand and lift the book. You blew air into the bag much the way you pump air into tires. Air pressure is so strong that large amounts can raise heavy trucks.

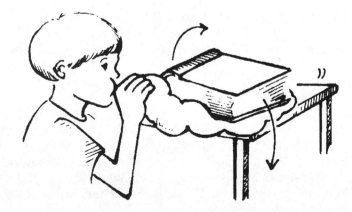

DUSTY AIR

What Is in the Air?

MATERIALS

flashlight

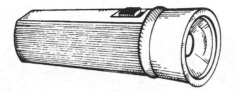

PROCEDURE

1. Turn on the flashlight.
2. Darken the room.
3. Direct the light beam on an object and look at the air space between the flashlight and the object. What do you see?

EXPLANATION

When you looked at the flashlight beam, you saw tiny **particles** (very tiny pieces) floating through the air. The earth's air is not just pure gas. It also contains particles of dirt, sand, cloth, metal, wood, plastic, ash, hair, and other materials. When the air becomes full of manufactured particles, such as soot, ash, or chemicals, we say it is **polluted**.

GUSTY GOING

Which Way Does the Wind Blow?

MATERIALS

scissors
ruler
piece of light fabric
stick about 1 yard (1 m) long

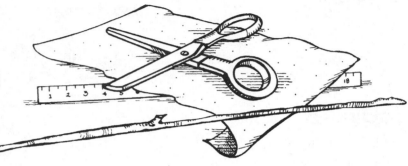

PROCEDURE

1. Cut a piece of fabric about 12 × 3 inches (30 × 7.5 cm).
2. Tie one end of the fabric to the end of the stick.
3. Go outside on a windy day. Push the stick into the ground, with the fabric on top. From which direction is the wind coming? How strong is the wind?

EXPLANATION

When the wind blows, air moves and pushes against objects. Your piece of fabric probably flapped in the wind and pointed in one particular direction, showing you which way the wind was blowing. The study of air movement is of particular interest to sailors and airplane pilots. This is why you sometimes see windsocks at airports or near water. They are there to tell you how strong the wind is and from which direction it is coming.

ANIMALS

 Most living things are divided into two main categories: plants and animals. The most obvious difference between the two is that animals can move around, whereas plants cannot. Most animals can see, hear, feel, smell, and taste, just as human beings do. Animals come in all different sizes, shapes, and colors. Some are huge, and some cannot be seen without a microscope. Regardless of the animal, each one is fascinating to study.

In this section, you will discover many things about animals. You will inspect a cat to find its claws. You will learn how to determine the age of a snail. And you will discover an unusual but interesting way of determining whether a turtle is a male or female.

CAT'S PAWS

Where Are a Cat's Claws When the Cat Isn't Using Them?

MATERIALS

friendly cat that has not been declawed

PROCEDURE

1. Observe the cat and see whether you can see its claws without touching the animal.
2. Gently examine the cat's paws. Try to find the claws.

EXPLANATION

When a cat is not using its claws, you cannot see them as you can see a dog's nails. When they are not being used, the claws are pulled back under the skin on the toes. When the cat needs the claws, the toes straighten and the claws come out. If the claws were always out, they would lose their sharpness when the cat walked on them. Cats use claws for climbing trees and catching their prey.

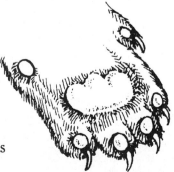

EGG SHAPE

Why Aren't Eggs Round?

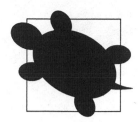

MATERIALS

hard-boiled egg
round ball

PROCEDURE

1. Place the hard-boiled egg and the ball on the floor.
2. Roll each one. Which one rolls more easily?

EXPLANATION

When you rolled the ball, it moved easily across the floor. The egg rolled a little, but mostly it just wobbled. Its shape keeps the egg from easily rolling out of a bird's nest; it also makes the egg more **resistant** (able to withstand) to breaking. A round object is more likely to crack than an oval one.

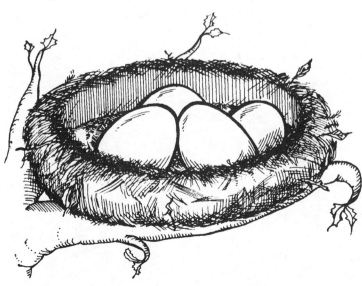

TURTLE EXAMINATION

How Can You Tell If a Turtle Is Male or Female?

MATERIALS

several turtles

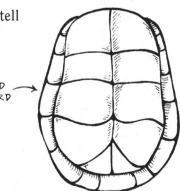

PROCEDURE

1. Gently turn each turtle over and inspect the shape of the under shell.
2. Find the curve of the under shell. Is it convex or concave?

EXPLANATION

The shape of the under shell can tell you whether the turtle is male or female. If the under shell, or **plastron,** is slightly **convex** (curved outward), the turtle is a female. If the shell is **concave** (curved inward), the turtle is a male.

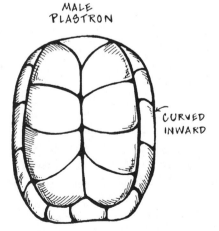

FEMALE PLASTRON

MALE PLASTRON

CURVED OUTWARD

CURVED INWARD

SNAIL AGE

How Can You Determine the Relative Ages of Snails?

MATERIALS

several snails
magnifying lens

PROCEDURE

1. Examine the snails under the magnifying lens.
2. Look carefully at each snail's shell. Look at the rings on the shell. Count the rings on each shell.

EXPLANATION

A snail is a **mollusk,** which is an animal that grows a shell to protect itself. When you examined the snail shells, you saw rings around them. As the snail grows, it adds new material to its shell. The shell grows at the lip, or edge, and more and more rings are added. Each ring represents a growth spurt. The number of rings you counted represents the number of growth spurts of the snail. Older snails have more rings around their shells.

SLOW FLY

What Happens to a Fly in Cold Weather?

MATERIALS

jar with a screw-on lid
hammer
nail
live fly
adult helper
You must have access to a refrigerator.

PROCEDURE

1. Ask your adult helper to punch holes in the lid of the jar with the hammer and nail.
2. Catch a fly in the jar and screw on the lid.
3. Place the jar in the refrigerator for a few minutes.
4. Remove the jar and observe the fly.
5. Remove the lid from the jar and release the fly outside.

EXPLANATION

When you placed the fly in the refrigerator, you caused its metabolism to slow down. **Metabolism** measures the rate of the chemical processes that take place in an **organism,** or living thing. Metabolic processes produce energy. The metabolism of the fly was slowed by the cool temperatures in the refrigerator, so the fly did not move as quickly as it did before. After the fly warmed up, its metabolism returned to its usual rate.

FISH SKELETON

What Does the Skeleton of a Fish Do?

MATERIALS

sheet of aluminum foil
fish skeleton, from a fresh
    fish market
magnifying lens

PROCEDURE

1. Lay the sheet of aluminum foil on a table and place the fish skeleton on it.
2. Separate the skeleton and examine the bones closely under the magnifying lens. Observe the long backbone, the individual bones, and the soft, bone-like substance that is between the bones.

EXPLANATION

Fish are called **vertebrates** because they have backbones. The backbone is made up of small, separate bones called vertebrae, which are separated by cushions of cartilage. **Cartilage** is a material like bone, but a little softer. You have cartilage holding up your nose. The long, sharp bones that extend from each side of a vertebra help to hold the fish's muscles in place. The backbone protects the fish's delicate and important **spinal cord.** The spinal cord, which extends from the brain along the back of the fish to the tail, is made up of nerve fibers. The sensitive nerves and cells of the spinal cord make up the nervous system, which is the control center for all of the fish's movements.

VERTEBRA

HELP HOLD
MUSCLES
IN PLACE

BACKBONE
(SPINAL CORD)

CARTILAGE

19

FRESH OYSTERS

What Is Inside an Oyster Shell?

MATERIALS

fresh oyster, from a fresh fish market
butcher paper
magnifying lens
adult helper

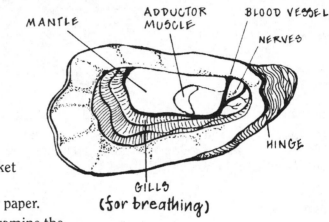

MANTLE
ADDUCTOR MUSCLE
BLOOD VESSEL
NERVES
HINGE
GILLS
(for breathing)

PROCEDURE

1. Have an adult at the fish market open the oyster shell.

2. Lay the oyster on the butcher paper.

3. Under the magnifying lens, examine the inside of the oyster.

4. Look for how the oyster opened and closed its shell. What do you think the other parts of the oyster are for?

EXPLANATION

An oyster shell is divided into two main sections. The first section is a hinge that allows the oyster to open and close as it gathers food. The second section, which is inside the shell, is a strong muscle called the **adductor.** This muscle attaches the oyster's body to the shell, so that the oyster can open the shell halves. Sometimes the oyster attaches itself to a rock or other object on the bottom of the sea. The oyster's shell is lined with a fold of tissue called a **mantle.** This lining grows from each side of the body and **secretes,** or gives off, a limy substance that makes the shell.

GRASSHOPPER PARTS

What Are the Parts of a Grasshopper?

MATERIALS

grasshopper
magnifying lens

PROCEDURE

1. Find a grasshopper in tall grass in your backyard or local park.
2. Examine the grasshopper under the magnifying lens.
3. Find the head with the antennae and large eyes.
4. Look at the middle part of the body and observe the legs and wings.
5. Examine the rear section.
6. When you have finished studying the grasshopper, release it outside.

THORAX

ANTENNAE

ABDOMEN

EXPLANATION

The grasshopper, like all insects, has three distinct parts. Its head portion includes a large pair of eyes and a pair of delicate **antennae,** or feelers, on the top and biting mouth parts on the bottom. The **thorax** (middle part of the body) has three pairs of legs and two pairs of wings. The third pair of legs, the thickest part, are used for jumping. The top pair of wings are long, narrow, and stiff. The lower wings are delicate, transparent, and fan shaped when open for flight. The **abdomen** (rear part of the body) has tiny openings in pairs that are positioned on each side of each section. A female grasshopper has a long, pointed, divided **segment** (section) at the end of the abdomen, called an **ovipositor,** for laying eggs in the soft ground. Males have bluntly rounded ends.

21

INSECT BUZZ

What Sounds Do Insects Make?

MATERIALS

live insect
plastic cup
sheet of wax paper
rubber band

PROCEDURE

1. Capture an insect in the plastic cup.
2. Place the sheet of wax paper over the top of the cup and secure it with the rubber band.
3. Hold the cup near your ear. What do you hear?
4. Remove the wax paper and release the insect.

EXPLANATION

Insects make sounds that are sometimes hard to hear. You could hear the sound of the insect because the insect was in the cup. The cup and the wax paper acted as an **amplifier** (a device that makes sounds louder). The air inside the cup vibrated with sound, which moved the wax paper and caused more vibration, so that the sound increased. Some insects make sounds by moving their wings back and forth. Mosquitoes flap their wings about 25 times a second, whereas honeybees move their wings 250 times a second. A common fly moves its wings about 120 times a second.

COLORS

 **Colors** result from different wavelengths of light bouncing off objects and entering your eye. All colors are found in white light. When light reaches an object, some wavelengths are **reflected,** or bounced back, and some are **absorbed,** or taken in. The wavelengths that are reflected to your eye are what you see as the color of an object. When you look at grass, you see green because the green wavelength is reflected to your eye and the other colors are absorbed.

In this section, you will experiment with colors. You will mix them together and take them apart. You can even create your own rainbow.

WATER RAINBOW

How Do Water and Sunlight Create a Rainbow?

MATERIALS

clear plastic cup
tap water
sheet of white paper
*You must have access to a
    sunny window sill.*

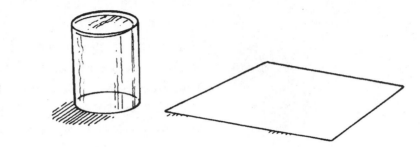

PROCEDURE

1. Fill the plastic cup with tap water.
2. Place the cup of water on a window sill in bright sunshine so the cup extends over the ledge a little. Balance the cup so it will not tip over.
3. Place the sheet of paper on the floor where the sunlight falls. What do you see on the paper?

EXPLANATION

A rainbow appeared on the sheet of paper. Although sunlight seems to be white or have no color, it is actually made up of all different colors. The combined colors formed a **spectrum,** or series of color bands. As light passed through the water in the cup, the light rays of each color in the spectrum bent in a different direction. When the rays were reflected on the paper, you could see all the colors of the spectrum as a rainbow. The order of the colors is always the same because the colors always bend the same way.

OIL RAINBOW

What Causes the Rainbow of Colors on a Patch of Oil?

MATERIALS

tap water
nonstick pan
eyedropper
vegetable oil
You must have access to a bright window.

PROCEDURE

1. Pour about 1 inch (2.5 cm) of tap water into the pan.

2. Place the pan on a table next to a bright window. Do not place the pan in direct sunlight.

3. Look into the water at an angle so the light from the sky is reflected in your eye.

4. Observing the water from the same angle, use the eyedropper to place a drop of oil on the surface of the edge of the pan closest to you. Observe the rainbow of colors that flash away from you toward the opposite edge of the pan. Watch what happens.

5. Blow on the surface. What happens to the colors?

EXPLANATION

When you first put the oil into the water, you saw a **rainbow** of colors spreading away from you toward the opposite edge of the pan. As you blew on the surface, the colors changed. The light rays bent as they passed through the oil, so you could see all the colors of the spectrum. As the oil moved, the light changed direction, so the rainbow swirled and bent.

SECONDARY COLORS

How Are Secondary Colors Made?

MATERIALS

scissors
ruler
blue, red, and yellow pieces of acetate,
  from an art supply store

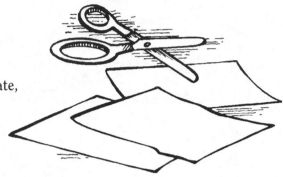

PROCEDURE

1. Cut two circles about 6 inches (15 cm) in **diameter** (distance across a circle) from each of the pieces of acetate.

2. Lay the acetate circles on one another to make additional colors.

3. Move the circles around to make as many different colors as you can. How many different colors can you make?

EXPLANATION

Acetate is a colored transparent material that allows you to mix colors easily and temporarily. When you put the acetate circles over one another, you created different colors. The **primary colors** are red, yellow, and blue. **Secondary colors** are combinations of two primary colors. All colors, except white, can be made by mixing the primary colors.

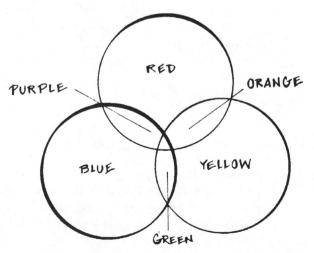

NEW MIX

What Happens When You Look Through Two Colors at Once?

MATERIALS

clear plastic cup
clear plastic bowl
tap water
yellow and blue food coloring

PROCEDURE

1. Make sure the plastic cup fits inside the plastic bowl.
2. Pour tap water into the bowl until it is about three-quarters full.
3. Mix in the yellow food coloring.
4. Pour water into the cup until it is half full.
5. Mix in the blue food coloring.
6. Place the cup of blue water in the bowl of yellow water. Look through the water in the bowl at the water in the cup. What color do you see? Test other colors by changing the color of the water.

EXPLANATION

The water looked green. Light is made up of a series of colored bands, the spectrum, which can be seen when light is broken apart by a prism. All objects reflect and absorb these colors, so the color of an object is determined by the color, or colors, that it reflects. The blue water reflected blue light and the yellow water reflected yellow light. All the other colors were absorbed by the water. By placing the cup of blue water into the bowl of yellow water, you temporarily mixed the two colors. This mixture absorbed most colors of the spectrum and reflected green light, so the water looked green.

BALLOON STRETCH

Why Does the Color of a Balloon Become Lighter When Air Is Blown into It?

MATERIALS

2 same-colored balloons

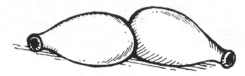

PROCEDURE

1. Inflate one balloon as much as you can without popping it.
2. Tie the neck of the balloon closed.
3. Hold the inflated balloon next to the balloon that is not inflated. What do you notice about the colors?

EXPLANATION

Balloons are made of an elastic material called latex that is colored with a **pigment.** By inflating the balloon, you caused the latex to expand and become thinner. This caused the pigment in the balloon to stretch so the color of the balloon appeared lighter.

HOT COLORS

How Do Colors React to Heat?

MATERIALS

sheet of black construction paper
sheet of white construction paper
2 thermometers
timer

PROCEDURE

1. Place both sheets of construction paper in the sun.
2. Place a thermometer under each sheet.
3. Read the thermometers after 10 minutes. What is the reading of each?

EXPLANATION

The **thermometer** (device for measuring temperature) under the black paper registered the higher temperature. Both sheets of paper were warmed by the sun's rays, but the white sheet reflected almost all the light that shined on it. The black paper absorbed most of the light. If you wear dark colors on a hot day, your clothes will absorb a lot of heat and you will be hot.

COLOR DYES

How Do Fabrics Respond to Different Dye Strengths?

MATERIALS

food coloring
2 small plastic cups
tap water
2 pieces of white cotton fabric
    about 2 inches (5 cm) square
2 paper towels
tweezers

PROCEDURE

1. Put two drops of the food coloring into each plastic cup.
2. Pour tap water into the first cup until it is three-quarters full.
3. Pour tap water into the second cup until it is one-third full.
4. Place one piece of the cotton fabric in each cup of colored water and let the water soak in for a few minutes.
5. Place a paper towel in front of each cup.
6. Use the tweezers to remove the pieces of fabric from the colored water. Lay each piece on a paper towel directly in front of the cup that it soaked in. What do you notice about the color of each piece of fabric?

EXPLANATION

By mixing water with food coloring, you prepared a **dye** (a coloring substance). Pure food coloring is a **concentrated** (not mixed with anything) solution. When you mixed in the water, you **diluted** the color, or made it weaker. The more water you mixed in, the more the solution was diluted, and the lighter the color became. When you placed the pieces of fabric in the dye, they absorbed some of the colored water, and the fibers turned the color of the dye. The piece that was in the more diluted solution came out lighter than the one that was in the more concentrated solution.

SPINNING COLORS

How Does the Eye See Colors That Are Moving Very Rapidly?

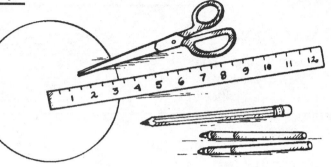

MATERIALS

ruler
pencil
cardboard circle
two different-colored marking pens
scissors

PROCEDURE

1. Use the ruler to draw a straight line through the middle of the circle from left to right and another line through the middle from top to bottom.

2. Use the marking pens to color each section of the circle, alternating colors.

3. Use the tip of the scissors to poke a hole in the middle of the circle. It should be large enough for the pencil to fit through.

4. Push the pencil point through the hole so the point is on the uncolored side.

5. Spin the pencil between your hands as you watch the colors. What happens?

EXPLANATION

When you spun the circle very fast, your eyes could not see the individual colors. Instead, they saw a color that is a mix of colors on the circle. The color that you saw depended on the colors of the marking pens you used. This is why movies seem realistic to us, even though they are made up of separate pictures. The film moves too fast for our eyes to see each picture, so we see the movie as a continuously moving scene.

CHROMATOGRAPHY

Can Colors Be Separated After They Have Been Mixed?

MATERIALS

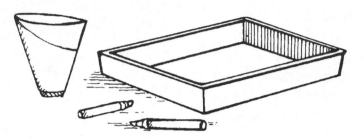

several different-colored,
    water-based marking pens
cone-shaped coffee filter
tap water
baking pan

PROCEDURE

1. Make as many different-colored dots as you wish on the coffee filter, keeping them about ¾ inch (15 mm) from the edge of the filter.

2. Fold the filter in half.

3. Pour tap water into the baking pan until it is about one-third full.

4. Stand the filter in the water, making sure the water does not touch any of the colored dots.

5. Observe the water move up the filter.

6. When the water has moved all the way up, remove the filter from the water and put it aside to dry. What happens to the colors?

EXPLANATION

Chromatography is a technique for separating chemical substances by taking advantage of the differences in the rates at which the substances are absorbed from a liquid. (**Liquid** is matter in a state in which molecules are able to move around, but are still held in contact with the molecules around them.) When you placed the coffee filter in the water, the water molecules were attracted up through the paper, which caused the inks to separate into the original colors that were combined to make them.

ENERGY

Energy is the ability to do work. When work is done, energy is **converted,** or changed, from one form to another. Energy can be taken from a number of sources, including the sun, oil, natural gas, and even wind and running water.

In this section, you will explore some of the types of energy we use to make our lives more comfortable. You will find out how to change one type of energy to another, and you will see how invisible energy can bend water and pop balloons.

HEAT ABSORBERS

What Types of Materials Absorb Heat Best?

MATERIALS

pencil
sheet of paper
*to be performed on a sunny
day.*

PROCEDURE

1. Draw a line down the center of the sheet of paper to make two columns. Label one column "warm" and the other "not warm."

2. Look around your indoor and outdoor environment.

3. Touch the objects that have been in the sun for some time.

4. List the objects that feel warm and those that do not feel warm in the appropriate columns.

5. When you have tested several objects, determine the factors the objects that warmed in the sun have in common. What do you find?

EXPLANATION

The amount of heat radiation absorbed by an object depends on what the object is made of. Dark, rough objects, like a rough, brown brick, are good heat absorbers. Light and smooth materials, like a white vinyl car seat, reflect most of the heat radiation. A dull, black object will feel much hotter on a sunny day than an object that is shiny and white. Scientists use this information to harness **solar energy** (energy from the sun) by making solar panels that collect and pass on the sun's energy. Solar power has many uses, including making a calculator work and heating a home.

HOT ICE

How Does Pressure Affect Energy?

MATERIALS

ice cube
paper plate
fork

PROCEDURE

1. Place the ice cube on the paper plate.
2. Press the fork into the ice cube and hold it there for a few minutes.
3. Remove the fork. What happens?

EXPLANATION

You can see how the ice melted. The top of the ice cube melted for an instant because of the pressure of the fork. The pressure of the fork caused heat energy to form. This heat melted the ice.

BENDING WATER

How Do Electric Charges Affect Water?

MATERIALS

tap water
comb

PROCEDURE

1. Turn the faucet on so a very thin stream of water flows from it.
2. Comb your hair for about 30 seconds or 30 times.
3. Hold the comb near the stream of water, but do not touch the water with the comb. What happens to the stream of water?

EXPLANATION

When you ran the comb through your hair, you charged your hair with static electric charges. The comb was charged with negative charges. Since negative charges attract positive charges, the charges in the comb attracted the positive charges in the stream of water, causing the stream of water to bend.

SUN BURST

How Powerful Is the Sun's Heat?

MATERIALS

balloon
magnifying lens

PROCEDURE

1. Inflate the balloon and tie the neck closed.
2. Hold the magnifying lens so the sun's rays are focused directly on a spot on the balloon. Hold the lens there until the balloon pops.

EXPLANATION

The sun's rays can be very strong. By using the magnifying lens, you concentrated the sun's energy on one spot and intensified the heat. The heat was strong enough to melt a tiny hole in the balloon, so the balloon popped. In hot countries, special curved mirrors, like magnifying lenses, are sometimes used to focus the sun's rays to heat plates used in cooking.

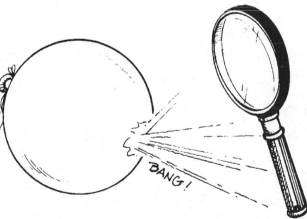

BANG!

37

BUTTON SPINNER

How Can Energy Be Changed from One Form to Another?

MATERIALS

3-foot (1-m) piece of string
large button with two holes

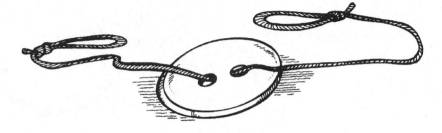

PROCEDURE

1. Lace the string through both holes in the button by going in one hole and out the other.
2. Tie the ends of the string to make large loops.
3. Move the button to the center of the string.
4. Hold one loop of the string in each hand.
5. Twirl the button toward you until the string is twisted tight.
6. Pull your hands apart and straighten the string. What happens to the button?
7. Relax the string. What happens when you continue to straighten and relax the string?

EXPLANATION

When you twisted the string, you transferred energy into the string, where the energy was stored. This stored energy is called **potential energy.** When you straightened the string, the stored energy was shifted to the button, and the button began to spin. This is energy of motion, or **kinetic energy.** The spinning button transferred the energy back to the string. As you straightened and then relaxed the string, the energy was changed back and forth between kinetic energy and potential energy. Wind-up clocks use kinetic and potential energy. When you wind a clock, you store the energy. As the energy is released, the clock runs, until the stored energy is used up.

WATER SPIN

How Does a Water Wheel Work?

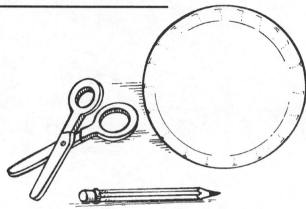

MATERIALS

scissors
paper plate
pencil
tap water

PROCEDURE

1. Cut a circle out of the paper plate about 4 inches (10 cm) in diameter.
2. Draw a circle about ½ inch (1 cm) in diameter in the center of the paper circle.
3. Make six 1-inch (2.5-cm) cuts around the edge of the circle. Be sure not to cut into the center of the circle.
4. Fold each of these sections in half so the folds stand up.
5. Stick the pencil through the center of the circle. You have made a water wheel.
6. Hold the water wheel's folds under a faucet and slowly turn the water on. You can turn the water on faster as you test your water wheel, but be sure to start off slowly. What happens when the water falls on the wheel?

EXPLANATION

When you held the water wheel under the faucet, it turned. Moving water can be used as a source of energy. A shaft attached to the wheel can be used to turn a system of gears. **Gears** are wheels with teeth around the edges that come together and turn each other. Gears can perform a variety of jobs. You may have seen old mills built on rivers. The millers used the energy from the moving river water to turn machines that ground corn and grains into flour.

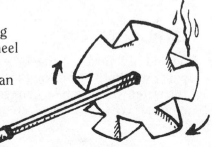

WINDMILL

How Does the Wind Produce Energy?

MATERIALS

pencil with a flat eraser
ruler
square sheet of paper
scissors
pushpin

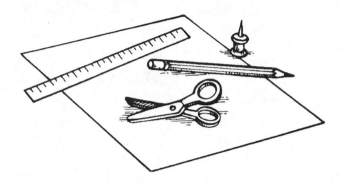

PROCEDURE

1. Draw a circle about 2 inches (5 cm) in diameter in the center of the sheet of paper. Put a dot in the center of the circle.

2. Cut a straight line from one corner of the sheet of paper to the circle. Be sure not to cut inside the circle. Do this for all four corners of the sheet of paper.

3. Bend every other point to the center of the circle without folding the paper. Hold the points there as you stick the pushpin through all of the points and through the center of the circle. You should have a paper windmill.

4. Gently press the pushpin into the pencil eraser.

5. Hold the paper windmill in front of you and blow on it. What happens?

EXPLANATION

A windmill moves by the force of the wind. You powered the paper windmill by blowing on it. To do work, the windmill, like the water wheel, can be connected to a shaft that turns a system of gears. Windmills can even power an electric generator.

EASY ELECTROMAGNET

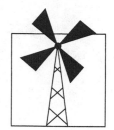

How Can You Make a Magnet with Electricity?

MATERIALS

scissors
14-gauge coated wire
screwdriver
ruler

4.5-volt battery
metal paper clips
adult helper

PROCEDURE

1. Ask an adult to cut a piece of the coated wire about five times as long as the metal part of the screwdriver.
2. Then your adult helper should scrape the coating off each end of the wire.
3. Leaving about 6 inches (15 cm) of wire at each end, wrap the middle portion of the wire around the metal part of the screwdriver so that the coils of wire are close together.
4. Wrap one end of the wire around one battery terminal.
5. Lay the paper clips on the table.
6. Place the tip of the screwdriver near the paper clips. What happens?
7. Wrap the free end of wire around the other battery terminal.
8. Again, hold the tip of the screwdriver near the paper clips. What happens?

EXPLANATION

When you connected the screwdriver to only one battery terminal and held it near the paper clips, nothing happened. When you connected the free end of the wire to the other battery terminal, the screwdriver attracted some paper clips. You made the screwdriver into an electromagnet. **Electromagnets** are magnets made with electricity.

RAISIN RAISING

How Does the Energy in Chemicals Produce Movement?

MATERIALS

tap water
clear plastic cup
raisins
spoon
2 tablespoons (30 ml) baking soda
2 tablespoons (30 ml) white vinegar

PROCEDURE

1. Pour tap water into the plastic cup until it is three-quarters full.
2. Drop the raisins into the cup.
3. Stir in the baking soda until it dissolves.
4. Add the vinegar. What happens?

EXPLANATION

When you first put the raisins in the water, they sank to the bottom because they were heavier than the liquid. When you added the baking soda and vinegar mixture, you made **carbon dioxide** gas. This gas made bubbles in the liquid, which attached themselves to the outside of the raisins. The bubbles helped lift the raisins, making them lighter than the liquid they were in, so they floated to the surface. After each raisin floated to the top, the bubbles popped and the gas went into the air. Without the bubbles, the raisins once again became heavier than the liquid and sank to the bottom to collect more bubbles.

GRAVITY

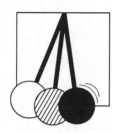

Gravity is the force, or power, that attracts objects to the center of the earth. It is also the force that keeps the moon in orbit around the earth and the earth in orbit around the sun.

Gravity makes rivers run to the ocean and fruits fall from trees. Gravity also allows you to walk, because it acts against the energy of your steps and holds you to the earth. It is one of the most mysterious and least understood forces of nature.

In this section, you will discover the power of gravity. You will learn how bridges defy gravity, how tightrope walkers balance, and even how gravity can help you hang wallpaper.

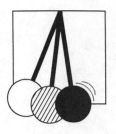

BALANCING ACT

What Is an Object's Center of Gravity?

MATERIALS

ruler

PROCEDURE

1. Hold the ruler vertically with one end in the palm of your hand.
2. Let go of the ruler and balance it upright for as long as you can. Can you feel a force pulling against the ruler?
3. Turn the ruler so it is horizontal.
4. Balance the ruler by placing the middle of the ruler on your finger.

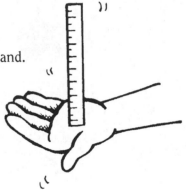

EXPLANATION

The steadiness of the ruler depended on how its **weight,** or its amount of downward force, is distributed. In order to balance the ruler, you had to find the center of gravity. The **center of gravity** is where all of an object's weight seems to be concentrated. It was difficult to balance the ruler when you held it vertically because most of the ruler's weight is at the top or on the bottom. When you turned the ruler to a horizontal position, you could easily balance it on your finger because the weight was evenly distributed on either side. Tightrope walkers depend on the center of gravity to help them balance on the high wire. They hold a long pole below their wrists as they walk on the rope. The pole lowers their center of gravity, making it easier for them to balance.

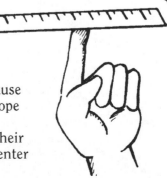

BALL GRAVITY

How Can You Change the Center of Gravity of an Object?

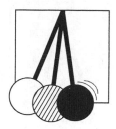

MATERIALS

tennis ball
flat thumbtack

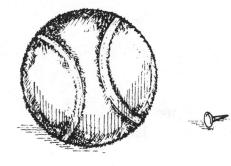

PROCEDURE

1. Roll the ball across a smooth floor.
2. Stick the flat thumbtack into the ball.
3. Roll the ball again. What happens when the ball rolls now?

EXPLANATION

In order for the ball to roll correctly, its center of gravity must be in the exact center. When you first rolled the ball, the center of gravity was always the same distance from the floor. This is why the ball rolled easily and evenly. When you stuck the flat thumbtack into the ball, you shifted the center of gravity away from the center toward the side stuck with the thumbtack. The ball did not roll as easily as it did before the thumbtack was added.

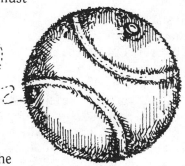

BOOK BALANCE

How Can You Make a Stack of Books Lean without Falling Over?

MATERIALS

6 to 8 books

PROCEDURE

1. Place one book about 1 foot (30 cm) from the edge of a table.
2. Place a second book on this book, but position it to extend over the first book just enough to balance.
3. Place a third book on the second book in the same way.
4. Continue stacking the books in this way until you have used all of the books. Be sure to balance the books so they do not fall over. What happens as you add books?

EXPLANATION

When you stacked the books in this manner, the books acted as though they were one object and stayed as a stack until the center of gravity was no longer supported by the bottom book. As you added each book, the center of gravity changed. But as long as the center of gravity was supported, the books did not fall over. When the center of gravity was no longer supported, the books tumbled over. Structural engineers use this knowledge when they design bridges.

GRAVITY BALANCE

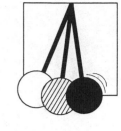

How Can You Make a Yardstick Balance at Different Points?

MATERIALS

book
yardstick (meterstick)
pennies

PROCEDURE

1. Open the book slightly and place it on a table, so the spine of the book is at the top.
2. Lay the yardstick (meterstick) over the spine and balance it.
3. Place one penny on one end of the stick so the stick tips.
4. Find the new center of gravity by moving the stick so it balances on the spine again.
5. Put a second penny on the opposite end of the stick. Now where is the center of gravity?
6. Continue to experiment by placing pennies at different points on the stick to find the different centers of gravity.

EXPLANATION

You can balance an object by supporting it under its center of gravity. The center of gravity is exactly at the middle of the yardstick (meterstick). As you added pennies, the center of gravity moved toward the end of the stick where the pennies were. When you added an equal number of pennies on either side of the stick, the center of gravity moved back to the middle. The large scales you see in doctors' offices work in a similar way by using a movable weight to counterbalance your weight.

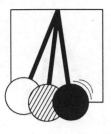

PERSONAL GRAVITY

What Effect Does Your Location in a Building Have on Gravitational Pull?

MATERIALS

bathroom scale
to be performed in a tall building

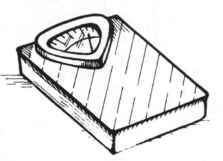

PROCEDURE

1. Weigh yourself on the top floor of the tall building.
2. Weigh yourself on the bottom floor of the building. Is there a difference in how much you weighed in both locations?

EXPLANATION

Weight is the measurement of the amount of downward force pulling on an object. Your weight on the top floor of the building was slightly less than on the bottom floor. Weight decreases as you move further from earth's gravitational pull. Astronauts are weightless in space because they are far away from the earth's gravity.

PENDULUM PLUS

Does the Weight of a Pendulum Affect the Timing of the Swing?

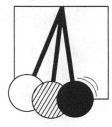

MATERIALS

2 pieces of string about 5 feet (1.7 m) long
3 spoons
2 pushpins
adult helper
to be performed in front of a doorway

PROCEDURE

1. Tie one of the pieces of string to the thinnest part of one of the spoons.

2. Lay the other two spoons on top of each other. Tie the second piece of string to the thinnest part of the two spoons together.

3. Ask your adult helper to attach the ends of both strings to the top of a doorway with the pushpins. The strings should be about 2 inches (5 cm) apart.

4. Keeping the strings straight, pull the spoons up to the same height and stand several feet to one side of the doorway.

5. Release all the spoons at the same time. Be sure they do not hit anything.

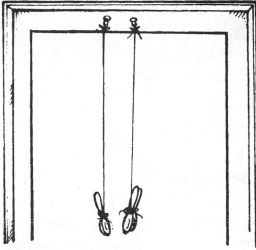

EXPLANATION

You made two pendulums. **Pendulums** are hanging weights that swing back and forth under the influence of gravity. When you released them, both pendulums moved back and forth at the same time with an equal amount of force. Both went back and forth to the same distance, even though one pendulum was heavier. Some clocks contain pendulums. The steady back-and-forth motion of the pendulum regulates the clock's movement.

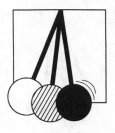

PENDULUM PLUMB

What Is a Plumb Line?

MATERIALS

piece of string about 3 feet (1 m) long
spoon

PROCEDURE

1. Tie the piece of string to the thinnest part of the spoon.
2. Hold the other end of the string so that the spoon points downward.
3. Wait until the spoon stops swinging.

EXPLANATION

A **plumb line** is like a pendulum that has stopped swinging. Plumb lines are used to find **vertical** (up-and-down) lines. Gravity attracts the weight to the center of the earth, making the weight hang vertically. Wallpaper hangers use plumb lines to make a straight line on a wall so they can hang the paper straight. Plumb lines can also be used to measure the depth of a body of water.

GRAVITY PULL

Why Don't Liquids Flow at the Same Rate?

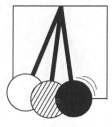

MATERIALS

paper hole-punch	large pan	vegetable oil
3 paper cups	molasses	timer
masking tape	tap water	helper

PROCEDURE

1. Punch a hole in the side of each paper cup near the bottom. Be sure the holes in all the cups are the same size and the same distance from the bottom.

2. Place a small piece of masking tape over the hole in each cup.

3. Place the cups in the large pan.

4. Pour the molasses, tap water, and vegetable oil each into a separate cup up to the top.

5. With your helper, remove the tape from the cups all at the same time. Note the amount of time it takes each liquid to run out of each cup. In what order do the cups empty?

EXPLANATION

The first cup to empty was the one filled with water. The last cup to empty was the one filled with molasses. While gravity pulls on everything with the same force, liquids may flow at different rates. The **viscosity** of a liquid is the rate at which the liquid can be poured. The thicker the liquid, the longer it takes it to move. Viscosity is also affected by temperature. Hot liquids flow faster than cold liquids. Pancake syrup spreads over pancakes faster when it is heated than when it is cold.

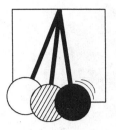

PENCIL FALL

How Does Gravity Affect Objects Falling at the Same Time?

MATERIALS

2 unsharpened pencils of different sizes

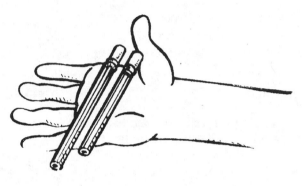

PROCEDURE

1. Place both pencils in the palm of one hand with the erasers pointing the same way.
2. Drop the pencils at the same time. Do the pencils hit the ground at the same time?

EXPLANATION

The pencils hit the ground at the same time. Size and weight have no effect on the time it takes for two objects to fall the same distance. Gravity pulls each pencil with equal force. The rate a free-falling object falls is 32 feet (9.5 m) per second.

THE HUMAN BODY

The human body is a complex organism made up of many different parts that all work together to help you function every day. Each cell in your body plays a vital role. The skeletal system supports your body with its detailed structure of bones. Your muscular system helps you move. Your circulatory system helps keep blood and other fluids moving. And your skin helps keep all of these systems inside your body.

In this section, you will discover much more about your body and how it functions. You will make an instrument for listening to your heart. You will tease your eyes with illusions. And you will even learn more about your family characteristics.

PULSE WATCH

How Can You Tell Your Heart Is Beating?

MATERIALS

toothpick
modeling clay

PROCEDURE

1. Stick the toothpick into a small ball of the modeling clay.
2. Hold your arm straight out, keeping it perfectly still.
3. Place the ball of clay with the toothpick facing up on the area of your wrist where you think your pulse is located. You may need to move the ball around until you find the strongest beat. What happens to the toothpick?

EXPLANATION

You saw a slight but regular movement of the toothpick. The toothpick moved as your blood was pumped on the long trip through your blood vessels to your heart. Your **pulse** beat because your heart moved as it pumped blood into the arteries for circulation through your blood vessels. Doctors measure pulse rates to find out if a person's heart is beating normally.

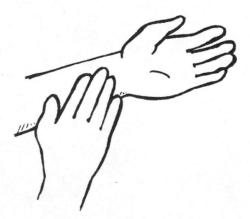

HEART SOUNDS

How Can You Hear Your Heart?

MATERIALS

2 plastic funnels
3 feet (1 m) of plastic tubing
  (that fits the ends of the funnels)

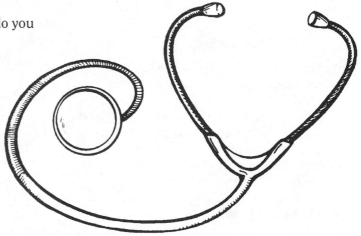

PROCEDURE

1. Push a plastic funnel into each end of the plastic tubing. Push hard so the funnels stay in place.

2. Place one funnel over your heart.

3. Put the other funnel to your ear. What do you hear?

EXPLANATION

You heard your heart pumping blood with this model of a stethoscope. A **stethoscope** is a device that captures sound waves and channels them down a tube directly into your ear so you can better hear sounds of the body. The funnel took in the sound waves over a large part of your chest.

MUSCLE BOUND

How Do Muscles Work?

MATERIALS

your body

PROCEDURE

1. Place one hand over the muscles on the upper part of your arm and hold it there.
2. Move the lower part of your arm back and forth. What do you feel?

EXPLANATION

Muscles are the part of your body that help you move. Muscles usually work in pairs. When you moved your arm, you felt your **biceps** and **triceps** working. Muscles like the biceps and triceps work when your brain tells them to. But other muscles move without instructions from your brain. For example, the heart is a muscle, but you do not need to tell it to pump.

BICEPS

TRICEPS

56

HAND INVESTIGATION

How Does Age Affect the Skin?

MATERIALS

magnifying lens
several adult and child helpers

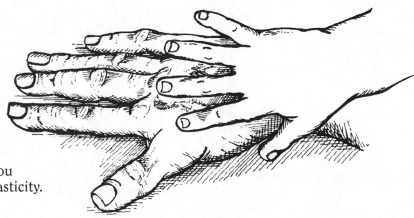

PROCEDURE

1. Examine the back of your hand under the magnifying lens.
2. Ask people of different ages if you can examine the backs of their hands. What are the differences between the skin of younger and older hands?

EXPLANATION

The skin is actually an organ of the body. Skin is elastic, so it expands and contracts with your body. As you get older, your skin loses elasticity. Like an old rubber band, the skin will not contract to its original shape. Instead, it becomes looser and tiny wrinkles form. When you look at an older person's hands, you can see where the skin has lost elasticity.

EYE LIGHT

How Do Your Eyes Filter Light?

MATERIALS

mirror

PROCEDURE

1. Look closely at one of your eyes in the mirror.
2. Notice the black spot at the center of the eye and the area around it.
3. Close your eyes for a few minutes. Then open them and look at the area around the black spot again. What does this area do when more light strikes it?

EXPLANATION

Light enters your eye through the little black spot called the **pupil.** Around the pupil is the colored part, known as the **iris.** If the light is dim, the pupil expands and lets more light in. If the light is bright, the pupil contracts and shuts out some light. When you first opened your eyes after you had closed them for a while, your pupil was large, but then it immediately became smaller as the light struck it.

PUPIL

IRIS

WEIRD WONDER

What Happens If You Stare at One Color for a Long Time?

MATERIALS

pencil
ruler
2 sheets of white paper
yellow, green, and black
   marking pens
timer

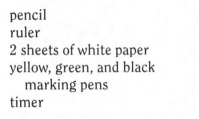

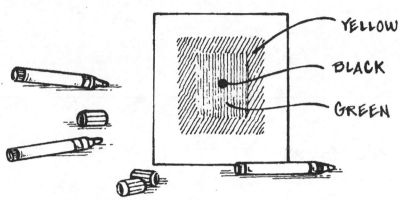

PROCEDURE

1. Draw a 6-inch (15-cm) square on one sheet of paper.
2. Draw a 1-inch (2.5-cm) yellow border around the square.
3. Color the area within the border green.
4. Put a black dot in the center of the square.
5. In bright light, hold up the paper and stare at the black dot for about 1 minute without blinking.
6. When time is up, look at the blank sheet of paper. What do you see?

EXPLANATION

You saw an image of the square on the blank sheet of paper, but in different colors. Special parts of your eyes, called **cones,** distinguish among green, red, and blue light. These are the three primary colors that make up white light. When you stared at the black dot for a minute, the cones corresponding to that color worked continuously. When you later stared at the blank white paper, which is made up of three colors, only the cones that were not working earlier worked because the others had been overworked.

CRYING EYES

Why Do Onions Make You Cry?

MATERIALS

onion

PROCEDURE

Peel the onion. What happens to your eyes?

EXPLANATION

When you peeled the onion, your eyes began to tear. Onions contain an irritating oil that escapes into the air when the onion is peeled or cut. This oil turned into a vapor that affected the nerve endings in your nose. These nerves are connected to your eyes, so when your eyes became irritated, tears flowed. To prevent tearing the next time, peel onions under running water. The water keeps the oil from spreading into the air.

FAMILY GENES

How Are You Alike and Different from Other Members of Your Family?

MATERIALS

pencil
sheet of paper

PROCEDURE

1. Write "Mom" and "Dad" on the sheet of paper.
2. Under each name, list some of that parent's obvious physical characteristics, such as eye color, hair color, and so on.
3. Then write your name and the names of your brothers and sisters.
4. List your own and your siblings' characteristics.
5. Compare your characteristics and those of your brothers and sisters with those of your mom and dad.

EXPLANATION

Genetics is the study of why living things look and behave the way they do. Inside each cell are tiny **chromosomes.** Different parts of each chromosome carry different coded messages. Each part is called a **gene.** Genes carry all the information needed to make a new plant or animal look and behave as it does. You get your genes from both your parents, and sometimes you can see which parent a characteristic came from.

OLD SHOES

Why Do Shoes Wear Out in Different Places?

MATERIALS

pair of old shoes

PROCEDURE

1. Examine the sole of each shoe for places where it has worn thin.
2. Look at the heels. Is one heel worn down more than the other?
3. Look at the toe area of each shoe.

EXPLANATION

When you pivot or walk, force is exerted on your shoe from your foot and the ground. This force causes your shoe to wear. When you examined your shoes, you noticed that they were worn in some places more than in others. These are places where you exerted more pressure, causing the shoe to wear more. Everyone's body is different, so everyone wears down shoes a little differently. Some people put more weight on the inside of their feet, whereas others put more weight on the outside.

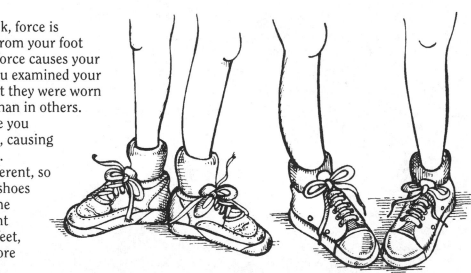

LIGHT

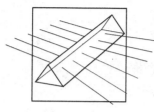

Light is a unique form of energy. It travels in waves that are always in straight lines. You see objects because light reflects from them. Light also magnifies, bends, and bounces.

In this section, you will discover why gems sparkle and why shadows change size throughout the day. You will even make a simple kaleidoscope using objects you collect.

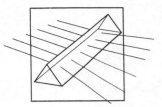

TINY MIRROR

How Does a Spoon Reflect Images?

MATERIALS

spoon

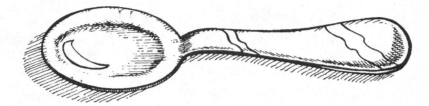

PROCEDURE

1. Hold the spoon by the handle and look into the bowl, which is the part that curves inward.
2. Turn the spoon horizontally and look at your image now. How does your image change?
3. Turn the spoon over and look into the part that curves outward. Now what do you see?

EXPLANATION

When you held the spoon by the handle with the long side of the bowl up, you saw a long, thin image of yourself. When you turned the spoon sideways, or horizontally, you saw a short, flat image. When you turned the spoon over, you saw an upside-down image. A spoon is both concave—bending inward—and convex—bending outward. A flat **mirror** (a surface that reflects most of the light falling on it) reflects, or bounces, light straight back to the eye, but a concave mirror reflects light toward the center of the eye. Since a spoon is not completely round, the light was reflected different distances, changing the shape of your image. A convex mirror reflects light away from the center and flips your image over.

MIRROR SERIES

How Can Light Be Reflected Several Times?

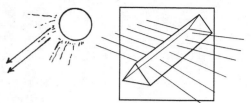

MATERIALS

5 or 6 mirrors

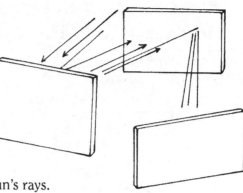

PROCEDURE

1. Place the first mirror directly in the sun's rays.
2. Place the second mirror where the sun's rays are reflected from the first mirror.
3. Place the third mirror where the rays are reflected from the second mirror.
4. Continue these arrangements until all the mirrors are used. What happens to the sun's rays when you arrange the mirrors in this way?

EXPLANATION

When you arranged the mirrors in this way, you caused the rays to reflect from one mirror to another, then another and another, and so on. When light hits a shiny surface like a mirror, the light rays are reflected in another direction. The rays reflect off the surface at the same angle at which they came in, so you can predict where the rays will go. You can use any number of mirrors to keep bouncing the light rays around.

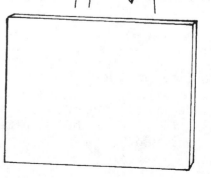

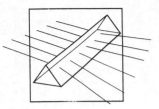

BENDING STRAWS

What Happens to Light When It Travels Through Water?

MATERIALS

clear plastic cup
tap water
drinking straw

PROCEDURE

1. Fill the plastic cup with tap water.
2. Place the drinking straw in the cup.
3. Bend down to look at the straw through the side of the cup. What do you notice about the straw?

EXPLANATION

When you looked at the straw from the side, it appeared to be bent, but it really was not. Light rays **refract** (bend) as they go from air to water. Light travels faster in air than in water, so the straw looked slightly bent where the light passed from one substance into the other.

LIGHT BEAMS

Why Does Light Make the Sky Look Blue?

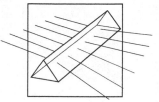

MATERIALS

clear plastic cup
tap water
milk
flashlight

 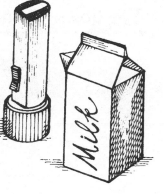

PROCEDURE

1. Fill the plastic cup with tap water.
2. Add a few drops of milk so the water becomes a little cloudy.
3. Darken the room.
4. Hold the flashlight in front of the cup so the beam shines through.
5. Look into the plastic cup from above. What happens to the milk?

EXPLANATION

When you added the milk drops to the water, the light became more visible because the particles in the milk reflected light. The light in the milky water turned pale blue because the particles separated out the blue waves of light. Dust and drops of water are almost always in the earth's atmosphere. These particles bend the light from the sun, causing the sky to look blue. When the sun rises or sets, the colors change because the light has to pass through more particles at different angles, so other light waves are bent toward your eyes.

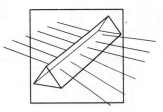

WEARING SPARKLES

Why Do Some Stones Sparkle in Light?

MATERIALS

cut crystal stone (such as a crystal
   bead or rhinestone)

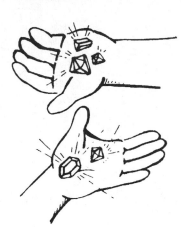

PROCEDURE

1. Place the crystal stone in the
   sun.

2. Move the stone around and examine how the light affects it.

3. See if you can make some sparkles
   bounce off the wall or floor.

EXPLANATION

Crystal beads and rhinestones are cut in
a special way to reflect the most light
possible. As the light hits the different
angles of the stone or bead, it is
refracted, producing a spectrum of color
and sending light back to your eye at
different angles, so the stone sparkles when it
moves.

STICK MIRROR

How Can You See Around Corners?

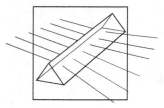

MATERIALS

yardstick (meterstick)
masking tape
pocket mirror
to be performed in front of a doorway

PROCEDURE

1. Lay the yardstick (meterstick) on a table.
2. Tape the top and bottom of the pocket mirror to one end of the stick. Be sure not to cover the reflective surface of the mirror.
3. Turn the mirror and stick over and tape the back to secure it better.
4. Stand on one side of a doorway and use the stick to hold the mirror out the door opening. Move the mirror around to see different objects in the environment.

EXPLANATION

You made a simple **periscope,** an instrument that lets you see objects around a corner. The light reflected off the mirror at the same angle at which it struck the mirror. If you held the mirror at the right angle, you could reflect the light rays coming through the door into your eyes, so you could see what was around the corner. Submarines use periscopes to look over the surface of the ocean.

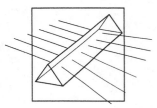

EASY KALEIDOSCOPE

How Can Reflections Be Multiplied to Make Interesting Geometric Shapes?

MATERIALS

3 rectangular pocket mirrors
masking tape
tiny objects (seeds, stones,
pieces of paper)

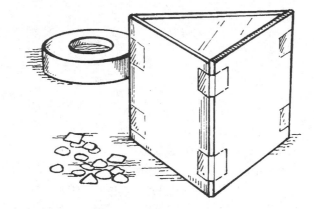

PROCEDURE

1. Arrange the three pocket mirrors so they stand on the short end and face one another. The mirrors should form a triangle with the mirrored sides facing in.
2. Fasten the backs of the mirrors together with the masking tape.
3. Drop the tiny objects into the space created by the mirrors and look through the opening at the top. What do you see?

EXPLANATION

You made your own **kaleidoscope.** Light in the kaleidoscope reflected from mirror to mirror, creating repeated images and patterns. When you changed the position of the objects in the kaleidoscope, new patterns of images were created.

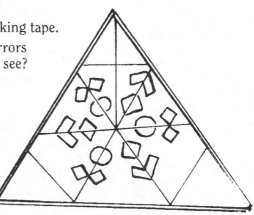

COMB BEAMS

How Do the Angles of the Sun's Rays Affect Their Strength?

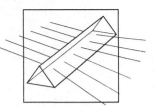

MATERIALS

comb
piece of white cardboard

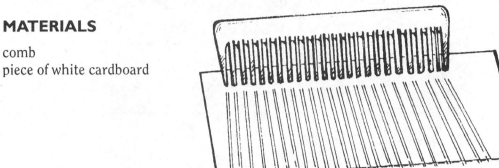

PROCEDURE

1. Place the comb with the teeth down next to one edge of the piece of cardboard so the rays of the sun shine through the teeth onto the cardboard.
2. Tilt the cardboard to different angles, always leaving the bottom edge next to the teeth on the table. How does the angle of the cardboard affect the light pattern on the cardboard?

EXPLANATION

Light can spread out or be concentrated to cover large or small areas. Depending on the way you tilted the cardboard, the sun's rays coming through the comb were either lengthened or shortened. When the light covered a large area, it was not as bright, because it was not as strong in any one spot on the cardboard as was the direct light. Because the earth is tilted in relation to the sun, light from the sun strikes the earth at different angles during the year. We have summer in our northern **hemisphere** when this half of the earth is tilted toward the sun and the light rays shine on it more directly. When it is winter in the northern hemisphere, the light rays hit earth at more of an angle and are spread out.

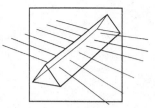

CHANGING SHADOWS

Why Do the Same Objects Cast Different Shadows Throughout the Day?

MATERIALS

flashlight
book

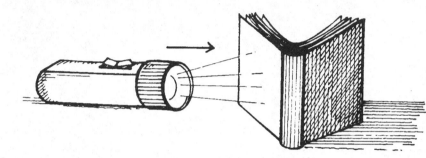

PROCEDURE

1. Turn on the flashlight and darken the room.
2. Place the book upright on a table.
3. Direct the flashlight beam directly over the book and look at the book's shadow. What size is the shadow?
4. Direct the beam at the book from the side. What size is the shadow now?

EXPLANATION

When an object blocks light rays, it creates a dark area called a **shadow** where the rays would have fallen. Shadows are predictable because light rays travel in straight lines. When you directed the flashlight beam directly over the book, the shadow that was created was short. When you directed the beam from the side, the shadow was long. On sunny days, shadows are long in the morning when the sun is low in the sky. Shadows become shorter and shorter toward noon, when the sun is almost directly overhead. When the sun sets, shadows become longer again.

MACHINES

Machines are devices that make work easier. They can be simple, like a level, or very complex, like a computer. With machines, people can perform many tasks they might not otherwise be able to do as easily or at all.

In this section, you will create a variety of useful and fun machines. You will make a simple submarine, a clock, and a machine that can move objects across the room so you do not need to get up.

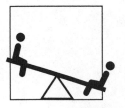

LEVER LIFT

How Can a Lever Help Lift Objects?

MATERIALS

book
ruler

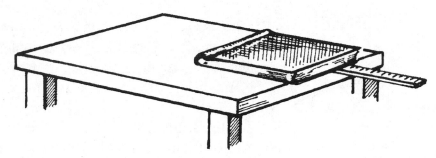

PROCEDURE

1. Place the book on a table so the edge is against the edge of the table.
2. Place the ruler under the book so the ruler extends over the edge of the table.
3. Slowly press on the part of the ruler that extends over the edge of the table. What happens to the book?

EXPLANATION

When you pressed on the ruler, you lifted the book. You created a simple machine called a lever. A **lever** is a straight, stiff object, like the ruler, that **pivots** (turns) at a point called the **fulcrum** (in this case, the edge of the table). Levers allow you to move an object using less force than you would need to move the object directly. When you push one end of the lever down, the other end moves up. The closer the fulcrum is to the object you want lifted, the easier it is to lift the object. Crowbars, nutcrackers, and even seesaws are levers. It is easier to lift your friend up on a seesaw than in your arms. If your friend moves closer to the middle of the seesaw, it is even easier to lift her.

EASY MOVE

How Can Wheels Be Used to Decrease Friction?

MATERIALS

2 books
5 drinking straws

PROCEDURE

1. Place one book on a table.
2. Place the five drinking straws on the table and place the other book on the straws.
3. Push each book with one finger to move it. Which book was easier to move?

EXPLANATION

The book that was on the straws was easier to move. The straws acted as wheels, reducing the amount of **friction** (resistance to motion) between the book and the table. There was less friction on the straws than on the book because a smaller part of the surface of the straws was touching the table.

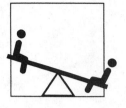

SINKING SUBMARINE

How Does a Submarine Float and Sink?

MATERIALS

2-liter soda bottle with cap
tub of tap water

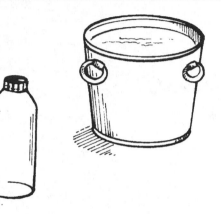

PROCEDURE

1. Place the soda bottle with the cap screwed on in the tub of tap water. What happens to the bottle?
2. Remove the bottle from the water.
3. Fill the bottle with water and screw the cap back on.
4. Again, place the bottle in the tub of water. What happens now?

EXPLANATION

When you first put the bottle in the tub, it floated. After you filled the bottle with water, it sank to the bottom of the tub. A submarine uses air and water in special tanks, called **ballast tanks,** to move up and down in the water. To dive, the submarine's tanks are filled with water. To rise, the tanks are filled with compressed air, which pushes out the water. A combination of air and water allows the submarine to stay at different depths of water.

SIMPLE SIPHON

How Does a Siphon Work?

MATERIALS

scissors
plastic tubing
2 plastic bowls
2 or 3 books
tap water
food coloring

PROCEDURE

1. Cut a piece of the plastic tubing about as long as your arm.
2. Place the first bowl on the books.
3. Pour tap water into the first bowl and add a few drops of food coloring.
4. Place the second bowl on the table. The tubing should reach from one bowl to the other.
5. Place one end of the tubing in the colored water. Suck on the free end of the tubing until all the air is removed and the tubing is full of water. Hold your tongue over the end of the tubing to keep the water in place.
6. Carefully remove the end of the tubing from your mouth and hold your finger over the end as soon as your tongue lets go.
7. Place the end of the tubing in the second bowl.
8. Remove your finger. What happens?

EXPLANATION

When you removed your finger from the end of the tubing, the water steadily flowed from the upper bowl to the lower bowl. This is how a siphon works. The water kept moving through the tubing once it started because the pressure of the air on the water in the upper bowl pushed the water up in the tubing. The weight of the water in the long end of the tubing pulled the water down.

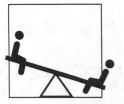

SAND CLOCK

How Can You Make a Simple Clock?

MATERIALS

two 2-liter soda bottles with caps
hammer
fat nail
sand

masking tape
timer
marking pen
adult helper

PROCEDURE

1. Ask your adult helper to put the soda bottle caps on top of each other and punch a hole through the center of both, using the hammer and nail. The holes should match perfectly.

2. Fill one bottle with the sand.

3. Place a cap on each bottle.

4. Hold the empty bottle upside down on top of the full bottle and tape the caps together tightly.

5. Flip the bottles so the bottle with the sand is on top.

6. Watch the sand begin to sift through to the empty bottle. Time how long it takes the sand to go through the bottle caps. Put a mark on the outside of the bottle at the sand level every 10 minutes.

EXPLANATION

You made a simple sand clock. The sand slowly moved through the cap of one bottle and through the other cap. The sand clock worked because sand always takes the same amount of time to flow through the hole. Many years ago, sand clocks were made by using glass bulbs. The sand flowed from one bulb to the other. They were called hourglasses, because it took exactly one hour for the sand to fall from one bulb into the other. Sand clocks are sometimes still used, for example, as small kitchen egg timers.

TURNING TIME

How Do Gears Work?

MATERIALS

2 large brass fasteners
large empty thread spool
small empty thread spool
piece of heavy cardboard
ruler
strong rubber band
marking pen

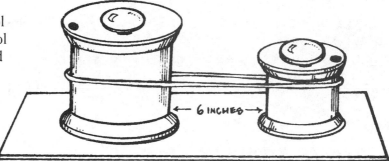

PROCEDURE

1. Put a brass fastener through the holes of each thread spool.
2. Use the fasteners to attach each spool to the piece of cardboard, 6 inches (15 cm) apart.
3. Stretch the rubber band around both spools so it is tight.
4. Mark a dot on the top edge of each spool. Turn one spool at a time and watch what happens to the other spool.

EXPLANATION

The diameter, or the distance across, of the small spool is smaller than that of the large spool. Therefore, you had to turn the small spool several times to make the large spool turn once. When machines use big wheels to move small wheels, the small wheels turn faster. When small wheels move large ones, the large wheels turn more slowly, but have more power. Gears are wheels that have teeth along the rims. The teeth fit into the spaces between the teeth in other gears, so when one gear turns, so do the others. See how big and small wheels work together by looking at your bike and its gears.

PULLING PULLEYS

How Can You Use Pulleys to Move Objects Across a Room?

MATERIALS

2 wire clothes hangers
2 empty toilet tissue tubes
piece of string the length of the distance
   between the door knobs, plus 6 inches (15 cm)
You must have access to two doors with door knobs across the room from each other.

large paper clip
tiny basket
adult helper

PROCEDURE

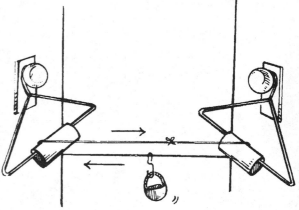

1. Ask your adult helper to unwind both clothes hangers and slip one wire hanger through each of the toilet tissue tubes.
2. Wind the wires as they were originally.
3. Suspend each hanger on a door knob.
4. Lace the piece of string around both tubes (where the toilet tissue was once wrapped), and pull the string so it is tight.
5. Bring the two ends of the string together and tie them in a knot. Cut off the ends of the string.
6. Bend the paper clip into a hook that has an S shape.
7. Place the S hook on the string and tighten it around the string.
8. Hang the basket on the bottom of the S hook.
9. Place small, lightweight items in the basket.
10. Pull the string. What happens to the basket?

EXPLANATION

You created a pulley system to transport lightweight objects. A **pulley** is a simple machine made from a wheel and a string or rope that helps move and lift objects. In this case, the pulley let you move an object so you did not have to get up and walk across the room in order to do so.

PULL UPS

How Can a Pulley Help Lift Objects?

MATERIALS

2 wire clothes hangers
2 empty toilet tissue tubes
tap water
plastic shopping bag (without holes)
piece of string
adult helper

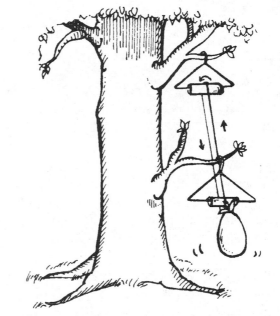

PROCEDURE

1. Ask your adult helper to unwind both clothes hangers and slip one wire hanger through each empty toilet tissue tube.

2. Wind the wires as they were originally.

3. Suspend each hanger on a tree branch or horizontal pole.

4. Pour tap water into the plastic bag.

5. Lace the piece of string around the tubes (where toilet tissue was once wrapped) and tie one end to the handles of the plastic bag.

6. Pull down on the other end of the string. What happens?

EXPLANATION

The pulley made it easy for you to pull up the plastic bag of water. The pulley changed the direction of the force needed to lift the water, so you could do the lifting job with less effort.

ROLL CAN

How Can Machines Store Energy?

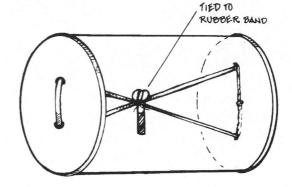

BOLT TIED TO RUBBER BAND

MATERIALS

can opener
coffee can
nail
ruler
2 plastic coffee can lids

scissors
long rubber band
piece string
bolt
adult helper

PROCEDURE

1. Ask your adult helper to remove both ends of the coffee can so there are no sharp edges.
2. Ask your helper to punch two holes about 3 inches (7.5 cm) apart in the center area of each coffee can lid.
3. With the scissors, cut the rubber band and lace it through the holes in the first lid.
4. Place this lid on one end of the can.
5. Cross the ends of the rubber band to form an X inside the can.
6. With the string, tie the bolt to the center of the rubber band.
7. Thread the two ends of the rubber band through the holes in the second lid.
8. Place the lid on the other end of the can.
9. Tie the two ends of the rubber band in a knot outside the lid.
10. Roll the can away from you. What happens when the can rolls?

EXPLANATION

When you rolled the coffee can, the bolt in the middle of the rubber band stayed in one place, but the rest of the rubber band turned and twisted. When the rubber band twisted as tight as it could, it stored all the energy put into it. When this happened, the can stopped rolling. The rubber band then started untwisting, releasing energy. This caused the can to roll back toward its starting place.

MAGNETISM

Magnetism is a force of attraction between certain objects. **Magnets** are objects that contain this force. We call objects that have the properties of magnets **magnetic.**

Through the experiments in this section, you will be able to "see" invisible magnetic fields. You will discover what objects magnets can attract, and you will see how the earth itself is one big magnet.

MAKING MOVES

How Do the Ends of Magnets Affect Each Other?

MATERIALS

2 bar magnets

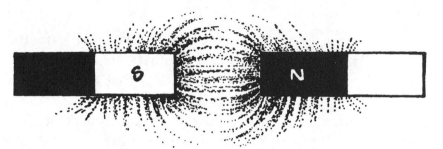

PROCEDURE

1. Lay both magnets on a table.
2. Slowly slide one end of the first magnet toward one end of the second. What happens?
3. Slowly slide the other end of the second magnet near the same end of the first magnet. What do you feel this time?

EXPLANATION

Magnets have **poles,** called "north" and "south," where the magnetic forces are concentrated. The magnetic forces move through each pole in a different way.

When placed near each other, the same, or "like," ends of magnets **repel** (push away) each other, whereas the opposite ends **attract** (pull toward) each other. When you moved the two like ends of the magnets close together, you felt the strong repelling force. When you moved the opposite ends close together, the magnets reached a point where they quickly attached to each other.

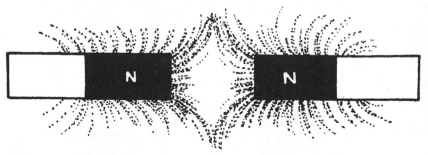

FILING FORCES

What Do Magnetic Forces Look Like?

MATERIALS

2 bar magnets
3 sheets of paper
iron filings, from a store that sells equipment for scientific experiments
ruler

PROCEDURE

1. Place one bar magnet on a table.
2. Put the first sheet of paper over the magnet.
3. Sprinkle some iron filings on the sheet. What shape do the filings take?
4. Remove the paper carefully and place the two magnets about 4 inches (10 cm) apart. The north pole of one should face the south pole of the other.
5. Place the second sheet of paper on the magnets and sprinkle some iron filings on the sheet. What shape do the filings take this time?
6. Remove the paper carefully and place the two magnets with their north poles facing each other and positioned about 4 inches (10 cm) apart.
7. Place the third sheet of paper on the magnets and sprinkle some iron filings on the sheet. What shape do the filings take?

EXPLANATION

The patterns of the iron filings revealed the magnetic field around the magnets. The lines you saw are called the **lines of force,** and they never cross one another. These lines in the field around a magnet reveal which poles attract each other and which repel each other. The first magnet under the sheet of paper showed an oval shape of iron filings. The north-to-south poles also showed the iron filings in an oval shape. The north-to-north pole showed the iron filings in a shape similar to a diamond. The same thing would have happened if the south poles faced each other.

85

NEW MAGNET

How Can You Make a Magnet?

MATERIALS

large needle
iron filings, from a store that sells
   equipment for scientific experiments
magnet

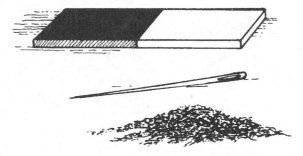

PROCEDURE

1. Hold the needle near the iron filings. What happens?
2. Rub the needle with the magnet about 75 times, stroking in one direction only.
3. Again, hold the needle next to the iron filings. What happens?

EXPLANATION

When you first put the needle near the iron filings, nothing happened. After you rubbed the needle with the magnet, the needle picked up the iron filings. An **atom** is the smallest part of a material that retains the properties of that material. When you stroked the needle with the magnet, you made many of its atoms move around and form a line. Magnets are formed when the atoms in a metal line up in the same way. By stroking the needle with a magnet, you lined up the atoms and made a new magnet.

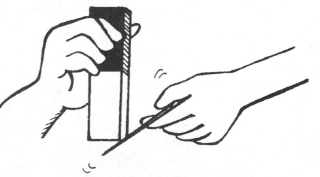

HOMEMADE COMPASS

How Can You Make a Compass?

MATERIALS

bar magnet
needle
plastic dish
tap water
knife (to be handled by an adult)
cork
adult helper

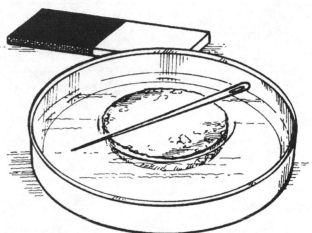

PROCEDURE

1. Rub one end of the bar magnet against the needle about 75 times, stroking in one direction only.
2. Fill the plastic dish with tap water.
3. Ask your adult helper to slice off a thin piece of the cork.
4. Float the cork in the water and lay the needle on top of it. Where does the needle point?

EXPLANATION

The earth itself is magnetic and has its own magnetic field. A **compass** is an instrument that detects that magnetic field. The south pole of a magnetic needle is attracted to the north pole of the earth, so it points to the north. By rubbing the bar magnet across the needle, you turned the needle into a magnet. The water allowed the needle to move freely.

WRONG READINGS

Does a Compass Always Give the Correct Direction?

MATERIALS

compass
large metal belt buckle

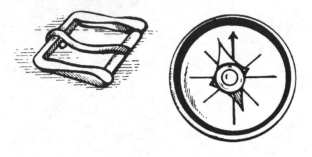

PROCEDURE

1. Use the compass to position yourself so you are facing north.
2. Place the buckle near the compass. In which direction does the compass point?

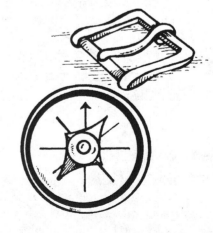

EXPLANATION

When you first read the compass, it gave you the accurate direction. When you held the compass near the buckle, the compass needle was attracted to the metal and gave an incorrect reading.

MAGNETIC DETRACTION

How Can Magnets Be Harmful?

MATERIALS

cassette tape
cassette player
magnet

PROCEDURE

1. Use a cassette tape that you will not need again. Play the tape for several seconds to hear the sounds on it.
2. Remove the tape from the player and rub a magnet all over the cassette for a few seconds.
3. Play the tape again and listen. What do you hear?

EXPLANATION

The first time you played the tape, you heard the sounds you expected. When you rubbed the magnet on the tape, the sounds were erased or changed. Recording tape is coated with an iron film. A recording is made by arranging the iron in the film in a precise manner that is detected or read by the recorder. The principle is similar to that of the changes in the width of the grooves in a phonograph record. A magnet pulls the iron particles out of alignment and destroys the recording. So beware! Magnets can destroy cassette tapes, videotapes, and computer disks.

MAGNET STRENGTH

Which Is More Powerful, a Bar Magnet or a Horseshoe Magnet?

MATERIALS

paper clips
bar magnet
horseshoe magnet (about the same size as the bar magnet)

PROCEDURE

1. Pick up as many paper clips as you can with the bar magnet.
2. Count the number of paper clips the magnet picked up.
3. Pick up as many paper clips as you can with the horseshoe magnet.
4. Count the number of paper clips the magnet picked up. Which magnet picked up more paper clips?

EXPLANATION

The horseshoe magnet picked up more paper clips. The horseshoe magnet can pick up about three times as much weight as a bar magnet of the same size because its two poles are so close together that their attractive power is combined.

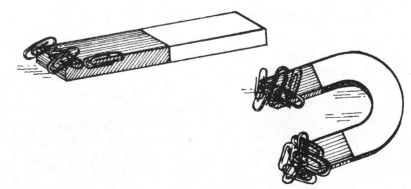

MAGNET CHAIN

How Can Objects Become Temporarily Magnetized?

MATERIALS

paper clips
bar magnet

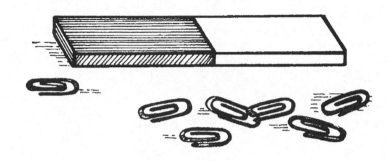

PROCEDURE

1. Place a pile of paper clips on a table.
2. Dip the bar magnet into the pile and pick up as many paper clips as you can. How many paper clips are being held up that are not touching the magnet?
3. Remove all but one paper clip from the magnet.
4. Hold the one paper clip over another paper clip. What happens?
5. Continue this process until you have a line of paper clips.
6. Remove the first paper clip from the magnet. What happens to the rest of the paper clips?

EXPLANATION

A magnetic force can be transferred through metals. This process enabled one paper clip to hold on to other paper clips as though it were a magnet. All of the paper clips that touched the first paper clip became temporarily magnetized. When you removed the paper clip touching the magnet, all the other clips fell off.

LIQUID ATTRACTION

How Does the Consistency of a Liquid Influence Magnetic Attraction?

MATERIALS

clear corn syrup
3 plastic cups
tap water
vegetable oil
paper clips
bar magnet

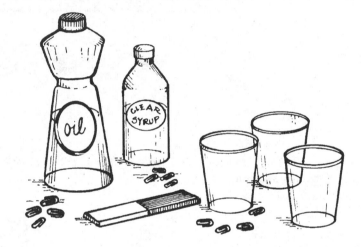

PROCEDURE

1. Pour the syrup into the first plastic cup, the tap water into the second cup, and the vegetable oil into the third cup until each cup is about half full.

2. Place at least 4 paper clips in each cup of liquid.

3. Move the magnet around the outside of each cup, trying to move the paper clips to the top of the cup. How do the paper clips react in each of the liquids?

EXPLANATION

In the water, attracting the paper clips was easy. When you tried to attract the paper clips in the vegetable oil, the attraction met with a little resistance. The paper clips in the syrup were the most difficult to move. These results show that the thickness of a liquid influences magnetic attraction.

MAGNIFICATION

Magnification is the process of making objects appear larger than they really are. Objects can be made to look much larger or just a little larger through the use of differently shaped lenses. A **lens** is a curved transparent material that bends rays of light. Lenses are used in a variety of instruments, such as telescopes and microscopes. Magnification allows us to learn a great deal about our world. It lets us see the tiniest living creatures, as well as stars that are lightyears away from earth.

In this section, you will discover how nature provides its own magnifying lens. You will also find out how eyeglasses, telescopes, and other magnifying devices work.

COMB RAYS

How Does a Magnifying Lens Affect Light Rays?

MATERIALS

4-inch (10-cm) circle cut out of cardboard
pencil
masking tape
comb
sheet of white paper
flashlight
magnifying lens

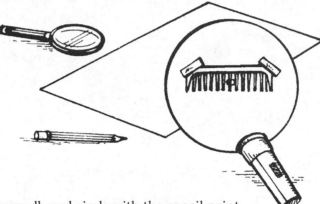

PROCEDURE

1. Poke a hole in the center of the cardboard circle with the pencil point and enlarge the hole with the pencil shaft.
2. Tape the comb over the hole.
3. Lay the sheet of white paper on a table.
4. Lay the flashlight next to the sheet. Position the cardboard circle between the flashlight and the sheet so the light shines through the hole.
5. Darken the room.
6. Hold the magnifying lens against the edge of the sheet so the light shines through it. What happens to the rays of light?

EXPLANATION

The magnifying lens is a **double convex lens,** a lens that is thicker in the middle than around the edges. It bends the light rays so they spread out, making an object look much larger when the light reaches your eyes.

DOUBLE CONVEX

How Does a Double Convex Lens Work?

MATERIALS

magnifying lens
sheet of white paper

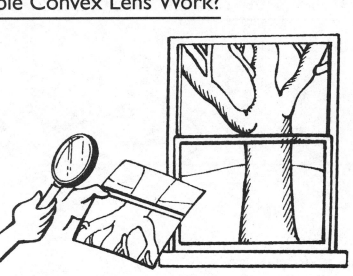

PROCEDURE

1. Darken all the windows in the room except the one at which you are working.
2. Hold the magnifying lens in your right hand.
3. Position the lens so it focuses on an object outside.
4. Hold the sheet of white paper in your left hand.
5. Move the paper slowly toward the lens until you see the outside object on the paper. What do you notice about the image?

EXPLANATION

The image on the sheet of paper was upside down. The magnifying lens is thicker in the middle than at the edges. This double convex lens caused the light rays that were approaching from different directions to meet at one point called the **focal point.** The light rays then continued past the focal point and crossed each other. By the time the light rays reached the paper, they were reversed. The rays that came from the bottom of the object were at the top, and those that came from the top of the object were at the bottom. To see an object right-side up through a magnifying lens, the object you are looking at must be closer to the lens than the focal point.

WORD FLIP

How Can You Make Words Turn Upside Down?

MATERIALS

book
2 magnifying lenses

PROCEDURE

1. Open the book and lay it on a table.
2. Place one magnifying lens on top of the other on the book.
3. Look through both lenses at the words on the page.
4. Slowly move the lenses toward you. What do you see?

EXPLANATION

The two magnifying lenses made the words look slightly larger when they were close to the book. As you moved the lenses away from the book, the words appeared much larger. When you moved the lenses still farther away, the words suddenly turned upside down. This happened because light rays bent by the lens crossed over each other beyond the focal point.

WATER MAGNIFIER

How Can a Single Drop of Water Magnify?

MATERIALS

piece of wire
large nail
plastic cup
tap water
newspaper

PROCEDURE

1. Wrap the piece of wire around the nail to form a loop.
2. Slip the wire off the nail carefully to keep the shape you formed.
3. Dip the loop into a cup of tap water so a drop of water is trapped in the loop. Examine the drop of water in the loop.
4. Hold the loop over the newspaper and look through the water. What happens to the print?

EXPLANATION

The newspaper print looked larger through the water magnifier. When you looked at the drop of water in the loop, you saw a bulge in the middle. This is the same shape as a magnifying lens. Water in a double convex shape acts as a magnifying lens.

ROUND WORKS

Why Must a Magnifying Lens Always Be Round?

MATERIALS

tap water
round glass salt shaker
square glass salt shaker
2 drinking straws

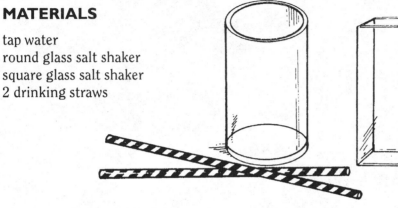

PROCEDURE

1. Pour tap water into the round and square salt shakers three-quarters of the way up.
2. Place a drinking straw in each shaker.
3. Look at the straws to see if they are both magnified.

EXPLANATION

When you looked at the round salt shaker, you saw that the straw was magnified. The square shaker did not magnify the straw. The curve of the glass acted as a magnifying lens. The light that bent toward the thickest part of the magnifying lens came to a point. The square shaker is the same thickness throughout, so it did not cause light to magnify.

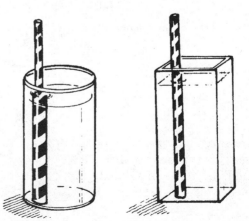

SHADOW LOOK

How Does a Magnifying Lens Affect Shadows?

MATERIALS

piece of white cardboard
plastic cup
ruler
flashlight
magnifying lens

PROCEDURE

1. Place the piece of cardboard on the floor so it is leaning against a wall.
2. Place the plastic cup on the floor about 8 inches (20 cm) in front of the cardboard.
3. Direct the flashlight beam on the cup and look at the shadow cast on the cardboard.
4. Place the magnifying lens between the cup and the cardboard.
5. Again, direct the flashlight beam on the cup.
6. Move the flashlight back and forth to get a clear shadow. Is the shadow larger or smaller than the shadow that was cast without the magnifying lens?

EXPLANATION

The shadow cast by the cup was smaller when the magnifying lens was placed between the cup and the cardboard. A shadow is the absence of direct light rays. When you placed the magnifying lens in front of the cup, it picked up the rays coming around the outside of the cup and bent them inward. Because there was more light, the cup's shadow was smaller.

MAGNIFYING MEASUREMENT

How Does the Distance of an Object from a Lens Affect the Object's Magnification?

MATERIALS

sheet of graph paper
magnifying lens
pencil

PROCEDURE

1. Lay the sheet of graph paper on a table.
2. Place the magnifying lens over the sheet.
3. Count the number of squares you see through the magnifying lens. (You can mark them off with a pencil.)
4. Move the magnifying lens up higher, toward your eyes, and count the squares again. What are the results this time?

EXPLANATION

The distance from a magnifying lens to an object determines the amount of magnification achieved or how large the object will look. As you increased the distance between the lens and the sheet of graph paper, you could see fewer squares, but they were larger.

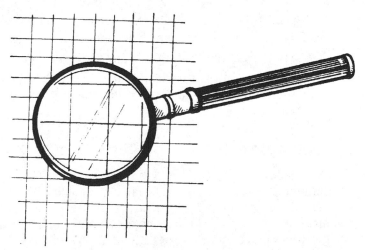

EYEGLASS LENSES

How Do Eyeglasses Help People See Better?

MATERIALS

several pairs of prescription eyeglasses,
  borrowed from friends

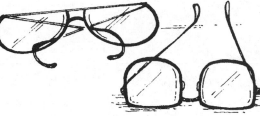

PROCEDURE

1. Try on one of the pairs of eyeglasses.
2. Look at a faraway object and a close-up object. How do your eyes focus on these objects?
3. Follow the same procedure with the other pairs of glasses.

EXPLANATION

Each type of lens helps correct a specific eyesight problem. Concave lenses are used for **nearsighted** people, who can clearly see objects close to them, but distant objects are blurred. This type of corrective lens is thinner in the middle than around the edges. It bends light rays outward before they reach the eye, so the rays focus on the retina instead of in front of it. A **farsighted** person can focus well on objects at a distance, but close-up objects are blurred. These people must wear glasses with convex lenses—lenses that are thicker in the middle than around the edges. Convex lenses bend the light rays inward, so they focus on the retina instead of behind it.

TELESCOPE IMAGE

How Does a Telescope Work?

MATERIALS

hand mirror
pocket mirror
magnifying lens
to be performed on a moonlit night

PROCEDURE

1. Lay the hand mirror on a flat surface by a window facing the moon.
2. Hold the pocket mirror in one hand so you can see a reflection of the hand mirror in the middle of it.
3. Hold the magnifying lens in the other hand so you can see the reflection of the moon in the pocket mirror. First look at the reflection of the moon in the pocket mirror, and then look at the moon directly.

EXPLANATION

The moon looked much nearer when you looked through the magnifying lens at the moon's reflection in the pocket mirror than when you looked directly at the moon. A **telescope** uses lenses and mirrors to collect and enlarge images of faraway objects. In this simple model, the magnifying lens enlarged the image in the mirror, but did not collect additional light. To collect additional light, a second, bigger lens would have to replace the pocket mirror.

WATER

Water is a colorless liquid that covers most of the earth's surface. It is essential to every person, animal, and plant. In fact, your body is made up of about 70 percent water!

Water has many interesting properties, which you will learn about in this section. You will discover how you can make water come out of the air, what makes objects float, and why ice is slippery.

WATER DROPS

Why Does Water Form Drops?

MATERIALS

clear plastic cup
tap water
spoon

PROCEDURE

1. Fill the plastic cup to the very top with tap water.

2. Add more water a spoonful at a time, trying to keep the water from spilling over the sides of the cup. What do you see when you look at the cup from the side?

EXPLANATION

When you looked at the cup from the side, you noticed a bulge over the top of the water. The water came up over the rim of the cup, but did not spill over the sides. The force holding the water in place is known as **surface tension.** This force causes water molecules to be attracted to one another and to hold together. An insect that appears to be walking on water is using the water's surface tension for support.

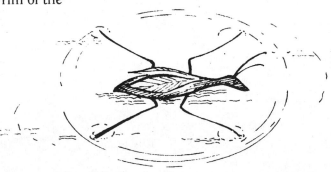

104

CIRCLE THREAD

How Can You Change Surface Tension?

MATERIALS

piece of cotton thread
plastic cup
tap water
dishwashing liquid

PROCEDURE

1. Tie the ends of the piece of cotton thread to form a loop.
2. Fill the plastic cup with tap water.
3. Wet the thread and place it on the water in the cup. What shape does it form?
4. Put one drop of the dishwashing liquid inside the loop. What happens to the loop now?

EXPLANATION

When you put the loop of thread into the water, it formed an irregular shape. When you added the dishwashing liquid, the thread moved out to form a perfect circle. The surface tension of the water is equal across the surface of the water. When you put the dishwashing liquid into the water, the surface tension inside the thread was weakened, so the tension outside the loop was greater than that inside. The surface tension outside pulled the thread into a circular shape.

WATER VAPOR

What Causes Water to Collect on the Outside of a Cold Glass?

MATERIALS

clean, dry glass
timer
You must have access to a freezer.

PROCEDURE

1. Place the glass in the freezer for 2 minutes.

2. Remove the glass from the freezer and wait 1 minute. What do you see on the sides of the glass?

EXPLANATION

There is almost always water vapor in the air. When you removed the glass from the freezer, warm water vapor from the air hit the sides of the cool glass. When the warm vapor cooled, it turned back into a liquid. The process by which a gas is turned back into a liquid is called **condensation**.

WINDOW FOG

Does Your Breath Contain Water?

MATERIALS

a window on a cold day

PROCEDURE

1. Place your face close to the window.
2. Exhale on the window. What happens?

EXPLANATION

You created a fog on the window. When you exhaled, you gave off a water **vapor** (a substance in its gas state) that you cannot generally see. Water condenses into a liquid when it hits a cold surface.

SLIPPERY ICE

Why Is Ice Slippery?

MATERIALS

ice cube
small, square wooden block about the same size as the ice cube

PROCEDURE

1. Place the ice cube and wooden block side by side on a linoleum or vinyl floor.
2. With one hand, push the cube and block together. What happens?

EXPLANATION

The ice cube traveled farther. This is because a thin layer of water melted under the cube. The water reduced the amount of friction, or force, on the surface of the ice. Friction reduces movement between one object and another.

SINKING SHIP

How Does a Boat Float?

MATERIALS

2 same-sized sheets of aluminum foil
tap water
2 plastic bowls

PROCEDURE

1. Form one sheet of the aluminum foil into the shape of a boat that has sides.
2. Crumple the other sheet into a ball.
3. Pour tap water into the plastic bowls three-quarters of the way up.
4. Place one piece of foil in each bowl. Which one floats? Why?

EXPLANATION

The boat-shaped sheet of foil floated, but the ball-shaped sheet sank. Both the density and the shape of an object affect the ability of an object to float. An object will float if the amount of water that is **displaced** (pushed out of the way) weighs the same as the object. An object will sink if the displaced water weighs less than the object. The object's shape will affect how much water is displaced. **Density** is the measure of an object's weight in relation to the object's **volume,** or the space the object takes up. An object that is denser than another object has more weight for the same volume. Objects that are less dense than water will float.

WATER WEIGHT

How Does Water Affect an Object's Weight?

MATERIALS

3 8-inch (20-cm) pieces of string
yardstick (meterstick)
2 bolts
2 plastic cups
tap water

PROCEDURE

1. Tie the first piece of string in the middle of the yardstick (meterstick). This will be the handle.

2. Tie the second and third pieces of string to each end of the stick, leaving 2 inches (5 cm) of string at one end of each piece.

3. Tie each bolt to the end of each 2-inch (5-cm) piece of string you tied to the stick in step 2. You have created a balance.

4. Fill the plastic cups with tap water.

5. Hold on to the string handle and watch the ends of the stick balance. If the ends do not balance, move the string handle along the stick until they do.

6. Dip one bolt into one cup of water. What happens to the balance?

7. Dip both bolts into the cups of water. What happens this time?

EXPLANATION

When you dipped one bolt into one cup of water, the balance shifted so that the bolt that was out of the water sank lower. Part of the weight of the bolt that you dipped into the water was transferred to the water, and the water helped hold the bolt up. When both bolts were dipped into the two cups of water, the bolts lost the same amount of weight and the stick was level.

LEVEL LOOK

How Can You Prove That Water Seeks Its Own Level?

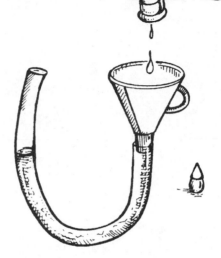

MATERIALS

plastic funnel
clear plastic tubing (that fits on the end of
   the funnel)
tap water
food coloring
helper

PROCEDURE

1. Fit the plastic funnel into one end of the plastic tubing.

2. Holding up both ends of the tubing, ask your helper to pour tap water into the tubing through the funnel until the tubing is about half full.

3. Ask your helper to add one drop of food coloring. Then shake the tubing.

4. Remove the funnel from the tubing and hold the ends of the tubing in different positions, with one end higher than the other. Notice the water level in each half of the tubing.

5. Continue experimenting with the positions of the ends of the tubing as you watch the water levels.

EXPLANATION

When you held one end of the tubing higher on one side, the water in the other side of the tubing shifted, so that the water level was always the same on both sides. The water level on one side never rose above that on the other side. Because this is always true, people say "water always seeks its own level." This is why people measure height on earth above sea level, because the sea is always the same level.

MAKING MONEY

How Can Water Create an Illusion?

MATERIALS

coin
plastic bowl
tap water
helper

PROCEDURE

1. Place the coin in the center of the plastic bowl.

2. Look over the rim of the bowl and slowly look down until you no longer see the coin.

3. Stay in the same position and ask your helper to pour tap water into the bowl until it is about half full. What happens as you watch the bowl?

EXPLANATION

As you watched the bowl fill with water, the coin seemed suddenly to reappear. This happened because light travels faster through air than through water. When the light passed from air to water, it bent. (See "Bending Straws," p. 66). The light reflecting off the coin bent toward you when it passed from water to air.

WEATHER

 Weather is the condition of the earth's atmosphere at a particular time and place. Many different factors make up weather. Some conditions of the atmosphere that can be measured are temperature, air pressure, wind speed, and moisture.

In this section, you will learn more about weather, the objects that help predict weather, and the effects of weather. You will learn how the location of thermometers affect their readings. You will create lightning. And you will even use a cricket as a weather forecaster.

WIND SAIL

How Does the Sun Affect Air?

MATERIALS

lamp without a shade
timer
baby powder

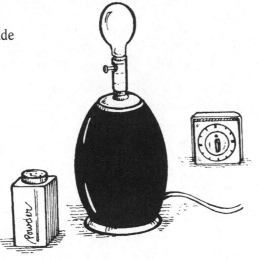

PROCEDURE

1. Turn on the lamp for about 5 minutes. *Caution: Do not touch the light bulb; it may get very hot.*
2. Sprinkle a tiny pinch of the baby powder above the light bulb. What happens?

EXPLANATION

The powder floated upward. When the light bulb warmed up, it also warmed the air above it. Warm air always rises. Every day the sun warms the earth and heats the air above it. Cool air moves down to take the place of warm air. This movement of warm and cool air masses is what causes most winds.

WIND DIRECTION

How Can You Instantly Tell Which Direction the Wind Is Coming From?

MATERIALS

your finger on a windy day

PROCEDURE

1. Wet your finger.
2. Hold your finger in the wind. What do you feel?

EXPLANATION

One side of your finger felt cooler than the other side. The cooler side was the side that faced the wind. The wind caused the water on one side of your finger to evaporate quickly, making your finger feel cool.

WIND WHEEL

How Can You Tell How Fast the Wind Is Blowing?

MATERIALS

pencil
paper plate
different-colored marking pens
4 small paper cups
stapler

long, thin nail
button
hammer
adult helper

PROCEDURE

1. With the pencil, mark off four equal sections on the paper plate.

2. With the marking pens, color each section a different color.

3. Place one paper cup on its side in each colored section ½ inch (1.25 cm) from the edge of the plate so the cups face counterclockwise.

4. Staple the cups to the plate.

5. With the nail, punch a hole through the middle of the plate.

6. Push the nail through a button hole and then through the plate.

7. Ask your adult helper to hammer the nail into a tree so the plate faces the direction from which you think the wind is blowing the hardest. Wait for the wind to blow and watch your wind wheel.

EXPLANATION

You created a simple **anemometer,** an instrument that measures wind speed. The wind pushed all the cups in the same direction, making the wheel turn. By observing how quickly the different colors blend together, you can see about how fast the wind is blowing.

WIND CHILL

How Does Wind Chill Affect the Reading on a Thermometer?

MATERIALS

2 thermometers
pencil
sheet of notebook paper
pushpin
timer

PROCEDURE

1. Read and record the temperatures of both thermometers.
2. With the pushpin, tack one thermometer to a tree on a cold, windy day.
3. Lay the other thermometer flat on the ground behind the tree.
4. Let the thermometers remain where they are for about 10 minutes.
5. Read the temperatures of the thermometers again. What did each reading indicate?

EXPLANATION

The thermometer on the tree in the wind registered a colder temperature because the wind took heat away from the thermometer more quickly than ordinary cold air does. The term **wind chill** was developed to account for the cooling effects of the wind on your skin. The stronger the wind, the lower the temperature adjusted for wind chill will be. For example, if the actual temperature outside is 25° F (14° C), but the wind is blowing at 20 miles (32 km) an hour, the temperature will feel as though it is –3° F (–20° C).

HUMIDITY CHECK

How Does Water Affect Temperature?

MATERIALS

2 thermometers
tap water
plastic bowl
piece of cloth

PROCEDURE

1. Take both thermometers outside.
2. Pour tap water into the plastic bowl.
3. Wrap one end of the piece of cloth around the bulb of one thermometer.
4. Place the other end of the cloth in the bowl of water.
5. Leave the other thermometer near the thermometer wrapped with the cloth and let both thermometers remain in the sun for a few minutes.
6. Read the temperature on each thermometer.

EXPLANATION

When the **humidity,** or the amount of water in the air, was low, the difference between the two thermometers was greater than when the humidity was high. When the humidity was low, the water from the cloth evaporated quickly, releasing heat and cooling the thermometer that you covered with the wet cloth. When the humidity was high, the water from the cloth took longer to evaporate because there was already a lot of water vapor in the air.

DEW POINT

How Can You Measure the Dew Point?

MATERIALS

thermometer
empty tin can with label removed
warm tap water
ice cubes
spoon

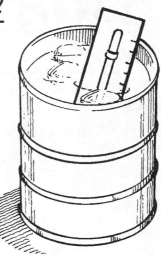

PROCEDURE

1. Note the air temperature outside the tin can.
2. Pour warm tap water into the can about three-quarters of the way up.
3. Place the thermometer in the can.
4. Add a few ice cubes, one at a time, and stir with the spoon.
5. Keep adding cubes and stirring until a mist forms on the outside of the can. *Note: Do not use the thermometer to stir.*
6. Read the temperature on the thermometer when the mist just begins to form.

EXPLANATION

The temperature you read is the **dew point.** As the temperature inside the can dropped, the water vapor touching the cold can also became cooler. This water vapor turned into liquid, called **dew,** and stuck to the can. At the same time, the air was evaporating the water on the outside of the can. At the dew point, evaporation was no longer taking place faster than the rate at which the water was sticking to the can, so the can stayed wet. The amount of water vapor in the air determines the temperature at which the water vapor forms on the side of the can. It also tells you the temperature at which dew will form on grass.

CREATE LIGHTNING

Where Does Lightning Come From?

MATERIALS

two balloons
wool mitten

PROCEDURE

1. Inflate both balloons.
2. Rub one balloon on the wool mitten and the other against a smooth wall.
3. Darken the room.
4. Hold a balloon in each hand and slowly move the balloons close together. What happens?

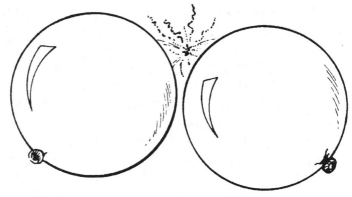

EXPLANATION

Every object has within it negative and positive electrical charges. Rubbing the balloons on the mitten and on the wall changed the charges of the balloons, so that one balloon had more positive charges and the other had more negative charges. When you held the charged balloons close to each other, the charges jumped from one to the other. The electricity created in this way is called **static electricity.** Electricity that jumps from clouds to the ground is called **lightning.** Electricity always jumps from negative to positive. Negative charges pile up at the bottom of a cloud and seek to reach the ground. When the difference between the charges is large enough, lightning flashes.

BAROMETER READ

How Does a Barometer Help Predict the Weather?

MATERIALS

plastic bowl
tap water
2-liter soda bottle

PROCEDURE

1. Half fill the plastic bowl with tap water.
2. Pour water into the soda bottle three-quarters of the way up.
3. Place your hand over the mouth of the bottle and turn the bottle upside down.
4. Place the mouth of the upside-down bottle on the bottom of the bowl. Remove your hand carefully and quickly.

EXPLANATION

This simple **barometer** can help you predict the weather. The air pressure inside the bottle stays the same. The changing pressure of the outside air on the water in the bowl causes the water level inside the bottle to rise and fall. Rising air pressure pushes water up into the bottle. Falling air pressure causes the water level in the bottle to drop. High pressure usually means better weather, whereas low pressure indicates colder temperatures or rain.

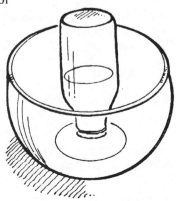

121

CRICKET THERMOMETER

How Can Animals Forecast Weather Conditions?

MATERIALS

crickets
watch with a second hand

PROCEDURE

1. Find a rural or suburban area some evening where you can listen to crickets.
2. Using the second hand on the watch, count the number of chirps a cricket makes in 15 seconds.
3. Add 40 to the number of chirps you counted to get a fairly accurate temperature in degrees Fahrenheit. (To determine what the cricket in your area can tell you about the temperature, you may need to use the centigrade scale. In that case, use this simple method: Subtract 32 from the number of chirps you counted, multiply by 5, and divide by 9.)

EXPLANATION

Many people believe the ways some living things react to the atmosphere are accurate weather forecasters. Accurate or not, these creatures are fun to observe. Other folklore weather forecasters include woodpeckers. It is said that when birds are very noisy, rain is on the way. When squirrels eat nuts in trees, the temperature will be very warm, and when pigs squeal in winter, a blizzard is coming.

Glossary

abdomen: rear part of an insect's body.

absorb: take something in.

adductor: strong muscle of an oyster that attaches the oyster's body to its shell.

amplifier: device that makes sounds louder.

anemometer: instrument used to measure wind speed.

antennae: delicate, long pair of movable parts on the top of an insect's head used for smelling and touching.

atom: smallest part of a material that retains the properties of that material.

attract: pull toward.

ballast tanks: air and water tanks that make a submarine move up and down in the water.

barometer: any instrument used to measure atmospheric pressure.

biceps: large set of muscles in the upper arm.

carbon dioxide: gas made up of carbon and oxygen.

cartilage: soft, bonelike material between bones.

center of gravity: point at which the whole of an object's weight is concentrated.

chromatography: technique for separating chemical substances by taking advantage of the different rates at which the substances are absorbed from a moving liquid.

chromosomes: tiny parts of a cell that carry genes.

colors: sensations produced by visible light entering the human eye.

compass: instrument used for determining directions.

concave: having a hollowed surface; bending inward.

concentrated: full strength; not mixed with anything.

condensation: change of the state of a substance from a vapor to a liquid.

cones: special parts of the eye that distinguish colors.

converted: changed.

convex: having a protruding surface; bending outward.

deflate: collapse by letting out air.

density: a measure of weight in relation to volume.

dew: warm, moist air that comes into contact with cooler objects, causing moisture to appear on them.

dew point: temperature on a thermometer when dew or vapor just begins to form.

diameter: distance across the middle of a circle.

dilute: make weaker.

displaced: pushed out of the way.

double convex lens: a lens that is thicker in the middle than at the edges.

dye: coloring substance.

elastic: material that returns to its original state after it has been distorted by a force.

electromagnet: temporary magnet that allows the flow of electricity through a wire.

energy: ability to do work.

farsighted: able to see distant objects better than close-up objects.

focal point: point at which lines of light come together.

force: power or energy that creates something.

friction: the force that resists motion between two objects rubbing against one another.

fulcrum: point at which a lever rests when lifting an object.

gears: wheels with teeth around the edges that come together and turn each other.

gene: small unit of a cell that passes characteristics from one generation to another.

genetics: the study of why living things look and behave as they do.

gravity: force that attracts objects to the center of the earth and keeps planets and other heavenly bodies in orbit.

hemisphere: half section of the earth.

humidity: amount of water vapor in the air.

ignite: set on fire.

inflate: put air into an object so that it expands.

iris: colored part of the eye around the pupil.

kaleidoscope: small tube of mirrors in which patterns are produced.

kinetic energy: energy due to motion.

latex: elastic type of material.

left valve: the part of the oyster that attaches to objects in the water.

lens: curved transparent material that bends rays of light.

lever: bar resting on a support that is pushed down at one end to lift the other end.

light: form of energy that is the source of illumination.

lightning: flash in the sky produced when electricity passes from one cloud to another.

lines of force: lines in the field around a magnet that show which poles attract and which repel.

liquid: matter in a state in which molecules are able to move around but are still held in contact with the molecules around them.

machine: any device that modifies a force so work can be done more easily.

magnet: a material that attracts certain other materials, such as metals.

magnetic: having the properties of magnets.

magnetic field: the attraction area around magnets.

mantle: fold of tissue lining an oyster's shell.

metabolism: process in living things that turns food into energy, new cells, and waste.

mirror: a surface that reflects most of the light falling on it.

molecule: smallest part of an element or compound capable of leading a separate existence.

mollusk: animal that grows a shell to protect itself.

nearsighted: able to see close-up objects better than distant objects.

organism: living thing.

ovipositor: long, pointed, divided segment of an insect's body at the end of the abdomen used for laying eggs in soft ground.

particles: very tiny pieces.

pendulum: weight hanging from a fixed point.

periscope: instrument that makes it possible to see around corners.

pigment: substance in things that gives color.

pivot: point at which something turns.

plastron: under shell of a turtle.

plumb line: device used to find vertical lines.

poles: north and south ends of a magnet.

polluted: unclean, impure, or dirty.

potential energy: energy that is stored.

pressure: force acting on each unit of area of a surface.

primary colors: yellow, blue, and red.

pulley: simple machine using rope and one or more wheels to change the direction of a force.

pulse: regular beating in the arteries caused by movements of the heart as it pumps blood.

pupil: opening in the center of the eye.

rainbow: arc-shaped band of colors.

reflect: bounce light off.

refract: bend light.

repel: push away.

resistance: ability to withstand a force.

secondary colors: combinations of two primary colors.

secrete: give off or release.

segment: section.

shadow: the dark area where light rays would have fallen if not for an object in the way.

solar energy: energy from the sun.

spectrum: a series of colored bands of light that can be seen when light is broken up, such as by a prism.

spinal column: long row of connected bones forming the backbone.

spinal cord: nerve tissue running down the spinal column.

static electricity: stationary electric charge.

stethoscope: instrument for listening to sounds of the body.

surface tension: force that attracts water molecules to one another and that holds the surface of water together.

telescope: optical device containing lenses and mirrors for magnifying distant objects.

thermometer: device for measuring temperature.

thorax: middle part of an insect's body.

triceps: small set of muscles in the upper arm.

vapor: a substance in its gas state.

vertebrates: animals with a backbone.

vertical: straight up and down.

viscosity: ability of fluids to flow.

volume: amount of space inside something.

weight: downward force exerted on an object by gravity.

wind chill: cooling effects of the winds and temperatures on skin.

Further Reading

Cash, Terry. *101 Physics Tricks* (New York: Sterling Publishing, 1991).

Frank, Marjorie. *202 Science Investigations* (Nashville, TN: Incentive Publications, 1990).

Glover, David. *Batteries, Bulbs and Wires* (New York: Kingfisher Books, 1993).

Glover, David. *Flying and Floating* (New York: Kingfisher Books, 1993).

Glover, David. *Solids and Liquids* (New York: Kingfisher Books, 1993).

Grafton, Allison, and Levine, Shari. *Projects for a Healthy Planet* (New York: John Wiley & Sons, 1992).

Hann, Judith. *How Science Works* (Pleasantville, NY: Reader's Digest Association, 1991).

Headlam, Catherine. *Kingfisher Science Encyclopedia* (New York: Kingfisher Books, 1991).

Herbert, Don. *Mr. Wizard's Supermarket Science* (New York: Random House, 1980).

Kendra, Margaret, and Williams, Phyllis S. *Science Wizardry for Kids* (Hauppauge, NY: Barron's Educational Series, 1992).

Kerrod, Robin. *How Things Work* (New York: Marshall Cavendish, 1990).

Kohl, MaryAnn, and Potter, Jean. *ScienceArts* (Bellingham, WA: Bright Ring Publishing, 1993).

Lewis, James. *Hocus Pocus Stir and Cook: The Kitchen Science Magic Book* (New York: Meadowbrook Press, 1991).

Lorbiecki, Marybeth, and Mowery, Linda. *Earthwise at Home* (Minneapolis, MN: Carolrhoda Books).

Mandell, Muriel. *Simple Science Experiments with Everyday Materials* (New York: Sterling Publishing, 1989).

Orii, Eiji, and Orii, Masako. *Light* (Milwaukee, WI: Gareth Stevens Publishing, 1989).

Simon, Seymour. *Mirror Magic* (Honesdale, PA: Boyds Mills Press, 1980).

Smithsonian Institution. *Color and Light* (Milwaukee, WI: Gareth Stevens Publishing, 1993).

Taylor, Barbara. *Green Thumbs Up: The Science of Growing Plants* (New York: Random House, 1991).

Taylor, Kim. *Structure* (New York: John Wiley & Sons, 1992).

VanCleave, Janice. *Janice VanCleave's Biology for Every Kid* (New York: John Wiley & Sons, 1993).

VanCleave, Janice. *Janice VanCleave's Earth Science for Every Kid* (New York: John Wiley & Sons, 1993).

VanCleave, Janice. *Janice VanCleave's Microscopes and Magnifying Lenses* (New York: John Wiley & Sons, 1993).

Watt, Fiona. *Planet Earth* (Tulsa, OK: EDC Publishing, 1991).

Williams, John. *Air* (Milwaukee, WI: Gareth Stevens Publishing, 1992).

Williams, John. *Color and Light* (Milwaukee, WI: Gareth Stevens Publishing, 1993).

Williams, John. *Water* (Milwaukee, WI: Gareth Stevens Publishing, 1992).

Experiment Index